CHETHAM & WOOLLEY
STONEWARES

1793 –1821

CHETHAM & WOOLLEY STONEWARES

STONEWARES

1793 – 1821

Colin Wyman

ANTIQUE COLLECTORS' CLUB

© 2011 Colin Wyman
World copyright reserved
First Published 2011

ISBN 978 1 85149 638 9

The right of Colin Wyman to be identified as author of this work has been asserted
in accordance with the Copyright, Designs and Patents Act 1988.

All rights reserved. No part of this publication may be reproduced,
stored in a retrieval system, or transmitted in any form or by any means electronic, mechanical,
photocopying, recording or otherwise, without the prior permission of the publishers.

British Library Cataloguing-in-Publication Data:
A catalogue record for this book is available from the British Library.

The publication of this book was made possible by a generous grant from
Ceramics-Stiftung, Basel, Switzerland.

Printed in China for
Antique Collectors' Club Ltd., Woodbridge, Suffolk, IP12 4SD

CONTENTS

ACKNOWLEDGEMENTS

This book is an assembly of information gathered so far by the author over some thirty years of research. During that long period much assistance has been generously provided by many past and present museum curators on both sides of the Atlantic and by individual ceramic collectors and dealers. Without their support the research presented here could not have been brought to its present stage (yet I am sure much more remains to be discovered about Chetham & Woolley). In particular I wish to thank Hilary Young and Robin Hildyard of the Victoria & Albert Museum, Dr Julia Poole of the Fitzwilliam Museum, Robin Emmerson, Myra Brown and Sue Lunt of the Merseyside Museums, Gaye Blake-Roberts of the Wedgwood Museum, Miranda Goodby of the Potteries Museum, Craig Berkely of York Museum, Pam Wooliscroft of the Spode Museum, Pam Judkins of Wakefield Museum, Jo Draper and Jerry Weber of Northampton Museum, Pat Halfpenny and Leslie Grigsby of the Winterthur Museum, Suzanne Hood of the Colonial Williamsburg Foundation, Nancy Franitza of the Nelson Atkins Museum, Amanda Lange and Peter Spang of Historic Deerfield, Massachusetts, Ulysses Deitz of Newark Museum, New Jersey, together with Paul and Melinda Sullivan, Elaine Chetham, John Mallet, Diana Edwards, Graham Hueber, Rodney Hampson, Warren Spencer, Michael and Nick Berthoud, Michael Chester, Geoffrey Frisk, Roger Pomfret, David Beaton, Harold Blakey, Tom Walford, Rosalind and Martin Pulver, Felicity Marno, Aurea Carter, Joyce Epps, and the late John Bentley, George Gittos, David Drakard, and Henry Weldon. All the better photographs are the result of painstaking work by Julian Cornish-Terrestral.

The publication of this book was made possible by a generous grant from Ceramic-Stiftung, Basel, Switzerland.

A further generous grant was made towards the cost of publication by the Marc Fitch Fund, England.

FOREWORD BY J.V.G. MALLET

Not so long ago it was fashionable for historians of British ceramics to sneer at the pioneer of their subject, Simeon Shaw (born c.1784-1786, died 1859). That his life ended in Stafford County Mental Asylum seemed to confirm the belief that almost everything he wrote was nonsensical. Writers able to draw on a hundred years or so of later research and publications give him little credit for having written his *History of the Staffordshire Potteries* as early as 1829, when no other published studies existed, so that he had to rely on memories and hearsay.

The more remote events are from one's own time, the less accurate to reminiscences of the kind tend to be. Thus, when collectors and historians of ceramics considered only seventeenth and eighteenth century wares worthy of study, Shaw's reputation stood at its lowest. Even for those early periods, however, recent research has quite often proved him wholly or partially correct.

When Shaw wrote of the early nineteenth century, that is of times he himself had lived through, he was on firmer ground. Thus, a brief but admiring paragraph about the partnership he described as 'Messrs. Cheatham [sic] and Woolley of Lane End', which he credited with having 'introduced into the market' around 1795 what he called 'a new kind of pottery, a dry body, without glaze or smear', known to contemporaries as 'Pearl', he should be taken seriously, not least because he wrote: 'Very few of the different attempts made to produce Pearl of equal excellence to the inventors, have been attended with any success.' However it is only now that the firm has found, in Colin Wyman, an author able to amplify very substantially what Shaw printed in 1829, and to identify many surviving products of the firm.

Wyman's book is centred on this white, dry-bodied 'feldspathic stoneware', for which he avoids the contemporary term in order to avoid confusion with 'Pearlware', essentially a creamware with a slightly blued glaze. When I first became involved with ceramic studies in the 1950s these white feldspathic stonewares tended to be known, generically, as 'Castleford', though even then it was becoming clear that other firms besides that Yorkshire pottery must have produced it. Heather Lawrence, in 1974, and Diana Edwards and Rodney Hampson in 1998, began serious study of these wares. It has, however, fallen to Colin Wyman to study in depth the few surviving marked pieces and the excavated shards and, by meticulous study of their sprigged ornament and other features, to identify numerous unmarked pieces.

The conclusions he draws suggest that, in both quantity and quality, Chetham and Woolley really were leaders in their field. Many times, when I worked in the Victoria and Albert's Department of Ceramics, I paused in front of the cherub head in Plate 156 of this book, wondering if it might not be, say, from Liverpool's Herculaneum Pottery. The model was familiar to me from earlier Chelsea porcelain examples, but the addition of wings and of the neo-classical plinth gave it a very different feel. The original seems to be a full-length statue of a boy, almost certainly due to the seventeenth century Italio-Flemish sculptor, François Duquesnoy. What I did not know, until Wyman's arguments persuaded me, was that this was a rare sculptural model produced at Lane End in the Potteries by Chetham and Woolley.

Colin Wyman does not concern himself much with other products of the firm, nor with ware made after about 1815, though the firm continued, if with less distinction, up to 1871. However there is much fine quality and varied interest in the ware he does describe and illustrate, with its combination of moulding, sprigged ornament and engine-turning, its restrained use of enamel. Rural sports and historical events of the Napoleonic Wars are recorded on it, mirroring the concerns of the clientele for which it was made. We are indebted to the author for opening up for us not only the story of an all but forgotten firm, but also for insights into the evolving technology of the Staffordshire Potteries and Great Britain's social life, as she entered the era of her greatest power and influence.

INTRODUCTION

James Chetham and Richard Woolley formed a partnership to make ceramics in the last decade of the eighteenth century and established their factory in Longton. The name Chetham appears on a delivery note from Wedgwood, which has the heading 'Newcastle' (referring to Newcastle-under-Lyme, the Staffordshire town close to Stoke) and is dated 16 November, 1791. The note is signed by James Chetham and acknowledges receipt of the contents of 'two hogheads'.[1] Although the name on the delivery is the same as one of the partners, there is always the possibility that there was another James Chetham living in Newcastle at that time, so it is not certain that the signatory is the same James Chetham who was in partnership with Richard Woolley. However, it has been established that from 1793 onwards the names Chetham and Woolley appear regularly together in local trade directories as partners in a pottery manufacturing business.[2]

Chetham and Woolley's factory was located in Commerce Street,[3] close to the famous and prestigious Turner family enterprise at the top of Market Street.[4] Commerce Street is in Lane End, a district of Longton which is the most southern of the pottery towns. The business was successful from the start, and the later descendants of James Chetham and his wife Ann, sometimes with addtional partners,[5] maintained a pottery business at the same Commerce Street location for nearly eighty years. It was only in 1871 that James Chetham's three grandsons, who had by then become the joint owners of the business, arranged for it to be sold. It was bought by members of the Aynsley family, who continued to make pottery on the site until well into the twentieth century. A section of the factory buildings still stands on the Commerce Street site in Lane End.

Although it is largely unrecognised today, the Chetham & Woolley Commerce Street factory once occupied a prominent position in the Staffordshire ceramic industry. It was particularly important in the period from the early 1790s to about 1820 and during this period it produced a distinctive range of wares of exceptional quality.

The success of the Chetham & Woolley pottery in these early years was in part due to the fact that, in about 1795, the founding partners had perfected a new type of ceramic material. From this they fashioned an extensive range of useful and ornamental wares which, according to contemporary sources, became universally admired.[6] The new ceramic material which Chetham & Woolley had developed was a special type of dry-bodied stoneware.

DRY-BODIED STONEWARE

The term 'dry-bodied stoneware' has become a useful identification for a wide range of distinctive ceramic bodies which were developed in the late eighteenth century, first by Josiah Wedgwood and subsequently by other makers.[7] Dry-bodied stonewares encompass the generic groupings of 'jasperware', 'black basalt' (sometimes referred to as 'Egyptian Black'), 'Turner ware', 'caneware', 'redware' (or 'Rosso Antico'), as well as the semi-translucent stoneware which is often referred to as 'Castleford ware'. The rationale for including such a wide spectrum of materials within the same terminology is that they all share many common characteristics. All are fired at high kiln temperatures to produce a dense, fine-grained, impervious body.[8] Stylistically, the wares are all similar in shape and design, and particularly in the applied sprig relief decoration which is a feature of all types of dry-bodied stoneware.[9] Many makers appear to have used the same sprig relief decorations interchangeably between the different categories of ceramic ware.[10]

Of all the dry-bodied stonewares, Josiah Wedgwood's jasperware is probably the best known. After a long period of experimentation, this material was finally perfected by Wedgwood in about 1776.[11] With the rise of jasperware Josiah Wedgwood's factory at Etruria in Stoke achieved high levels of artistry. Strikingly stylish vases and other ornamental and useful wares were created by placing a fine white sprig relief decoration onto elegantly shaped jasperware forms of a contrasting background colour, most notably 'Wedgwood blue'. Josiah Wedgwood's jasper-ware was much admired in the fashionable circles of his time[12] and an enthusiastic market for it was created throughout Europe amongst a discerning and even princely clientele.[13] The appeal of jasperware survives to the present day.

However, jasperware was not the only dry-bodied stoneware which Josiah Wedgwood had perfected. In the previous decade he had greatly refined and transformed a black stoneware body known as Egyptian Black which had existed for some time. Wedgwood exploited the improve-ments he made to the early formulas with great

success and he gave it the name 'black basalt'. Josiah Wedgwood himself was delighted with black basalt and in letters to his friend and business partner, Thomas Bentley, he often referred enthusiastically to the pressing demand from his distinguished clientele for basalt vases.[14] Indeed, in the 1760's he could scarcely produce enough to keep up with the market.

Black basalt was the first dry-bodied stoneware from which Wedgwood crafted his elegant vases and other stylish objects and the shapes were often taken from antique classical models. The majority of black basalt vases were decorated with applied sprig relief mouldings which were also commonly derived from classical sources.[15] The demand amongst aristocratic society for Wedgwood's basalt antique vases established his reputation as a potter of refined taste. He therefore already had an existing supportive clientele of aristocratic patrons (as well as those lower in the social scale who emulated their taste) to whom he was later able to introduce jasperware and his other innovations. By constantly perfecting or inventing new ceramic materials and consistently fashioning new elegant decorative wares Josiah Wedgwood became one of the best known and most successful potters of his age.

Although Wedgwood made many of the most important contributions to the development of the various types of dry-bodied stoneware, he did not long remain their only maker and competitors soon appeared.[16] John Turner, an exceptionally talented potter with a factory very close to the Chetham & Woolley's factory in Lane End, was probably the first to present a serious challenge. Working alone and later with his two sons, William and John, he also produced basalt and jasper stonewares, all of the finest quality and comparable in every way to those made by Josiah Wedgwood.[17] The Turner factory also developed a unique dry-bodied stoneware which did not appear at all in Wedgwood's repertoire. This special material was said to be made from a particular vein of clay that John Turner had discovered c.1780.[18] This stoneware from the Turner factory has an exquisite honey colour and with it they produced a beautiful range of sprig relief decorated jugs, mugs, teapots, vases and other wares. The term 'Turner ware' is now commonly used to describe this fine material and pieces are commonly marked on the base with the Turner name in impressed capital letters.

By 1800 there were a host of substantial, good quality, highly productive manufacturers all competing for the biggest market share of sprig relief decorated fine dry-bodied stoneware. Successful manufacturers such as Spode, Davenport, Wilson, Elijah Mayer, the Hollins family, Warburton and Dunderdale were just some of the many firms involved. These factories all made black basalt and some made jasperware as well. Of particular interest is the fact that, by 1800, many of these factories had also begun to produce different versions of another new type of dry-bodied stoneware. This new material had the special feature of being semi-translucent or 'porcellaneous' and it became a very important addition to the dry-bodied stoneware range.[19]

The most accurate term used to identify this new material is 'feldspathic stoneware'. It was in Staffordshire that the new feldspathic stoneware products were most widely developed.

Unusually, the Wedgwood factory appears not to have led the early development of feldspathic stoneware. Although by the mid 1770s a stoneware known as 'white terracotta' was being made by his factory, this body does not have the same translucency as feldspathic stoneware, but it may have had an influence on the development of the latter material. It is possible that following the death of Josiah Wedgwood in 1795, his heirs may have been either less devoted or less able to pursue product innovation to the same extent.

It was approximately in the year of Josiah Wedgwood's death that the new semi-translucent feldspathic stoneware first appeared. Although it may have had some similarity to Wedgwood's white terracotta, it was presented to the market as an entirely new body and rapidly became an important feature of the dry-bodied stoneware range. By 1800 many manufacturers were making different versions of the new material and the production of jugs, mugs, teapots, creamers and other useful wares was widespread. Not surprisingly, the most extensive range of items made from feldspathic stoneware, including attractive ornamental wares, emanated from the reputed inventors of the material, Messrs. Chetham & Woolley of Lane End. Their range of dry-bodied feldspathic products can be classified according to the following groupings:

1. The Oak-leaf Border Group
2. Pearl Stoneware Jugs
3. Pearl Stoneware Mugs
4. Pratt-type Wares
5. Mist-type Wares
6. Miscellaneous

Each of these groups are examined in later chapters of this book.

1.

FELDSPATHIC STONEWARE

Feldspathic Stoneware was first introduced to the market in c.1795 by Chetham & Woolley, and it quickly became an important addition to the range of ceramic materials used by the potteries. In order to consider the importance of this type of stoneware, a brief discussion of a fundamental distinction in pottery ceramics is required.

A widely acknowledged classification of pottery ceramics divides wares into two main groupings: earthenware and porcelain. Earthenware is the earliest form of pottery and dates back to at least the Egyptian and Mesopotamian cultures, though it undoubtedly existed in a less sophisticated state before then. Porcelain, on the other hand, is a relatively new material and was developed in China just over one thousand years ago. The secret of making porcelain was unknown in the West until it was finally discovered by Bottger, who worked at Meissen in the early years of the eighteenth century.

One of the most commonly recommended procedures for distinguishing earthenware from porcelain is the test of translucency. If held against a light source, earthenware is opaque, whereas porcelain will allow light to shine through. In this respect, porcelain has some association to glass, a relationship which is not shared by earthenware. Although not always appropriate, this simple translucency test is generally a useful way of distinguishing between the two materials.

There are also other differences between the two types of ceramics. One of the most basic distinctions comes from the fact that the mixture of clays which is used to make earthenware is different from that used for porcelain. If the structure of earthenware is examined under magnification, it reveals a grainy appearance, sometimes of a rough and discontinuous character. Porcelain, by contrast, has a much finer, glassy appearance and, as a result, is generally described as a vitrified material.

A most important property which coincides with these differences in the structure of the two materials is their reaction to liquids. If liquids are put into a porcelain vessel, the fine glassy structure will not absorb it to any significant degree. On the other hand, an earthenware vessel with its grainy structure will absorb some of the liquid because in its simple form it is porous. Therefore, in order for earthenware vessels to hold liquids without absorbing them the containers must be glazed.

These important distinctions between earthenware and porcelain are not simply achieved by using special mixes of clay. Although this is vital, the temperature at which the clay is fired in the kiln is equally important. Earthenware is fired at a relatively low temperature (approximately 800-950°C), whereas porcelain must be fired at a much higher temperature, in excess of about 1,150°C. If the correct porcelain clay mixture was fired at the lower earthenware temperatures, the result would not be a success; the physics are just as important as the chemistry.

The two-pronged classification of pottery into either earthenware or porcelain is complicated by the existence of a third ceramic material: stoneware.

Stoneware was first developed in China prior to the development of porcelain, and the clay mix for stoneware is not the same. Stoneware is more like earthenware, but differs from simple earthenware formulae in that the clays for stoneware are capable of withstanding high temperature firing. The essential point is that stoneware bodies are not fired at the low temperatures associated with earthenware production, but at the high temperatures which are commonly required for porcelain. The resulting stoneware body is a fine-grained, dense, vitrified material which, like porcelain, will not absorb liquids. Stoneware does not need to be glazed in order to hold liquids, but it is like earthenware to the extent

that it is generally opaque in its simple form. For this reason, stoneware is widely (some would say wrongly) categorised with earthenware. It might, perhaps, be more accurate to consider it an intermediary yet separate ceramic category between earthenware and porcelain.

The claim for separate categorisation is reinforced by the development of a later material known as 'Feldspathic Stoneware'. Feldspar is a naturally occuring mineral associated with granite rock formations. It is found in various stages of decomposition, one form of which is the famous Chinese Kaolin, or china clay. Feldspatic clays have always been widely used in the manufacture of porcelain where the feldspar acts as a flux to facilitate vitrification.

A fascinating step in the development of ceramic bodies occured when feldspatic clays were first added in greater proportions to the stoneware formula. When this is done and the clays are fired at high kiln temperatures, the result is not only a stoneware which has all the normal properties described above, but a stoneware which is no longer opaque. A considerable amount of light can pass through this special stoneware, although the amount is not as great as that which shows through porcelain.

As a result, this special stoneware with the extra feldspar is sometimes called 'Semi-translucent Stoneware'. Because translucency is a feature of porcelain, it is also known as 'Porcellaneous Stoneware'. Strictly speaking, the correct term is 'Feldspathic Stoneware', though all three terms refer to the same material.

Some of the interesting qualities of this new material can be seen in the representation of Admiral Lord Nelson (Plate 57a), where a light has been placed inside a Chetham & Woolley feldspathic stoneware jug of c.1806.

2.

Market Conditions for Decorative Ceramics in the Late Eighteenth Century

It is an intriguing truism that none of the abundant examples of late eighteenth century stoneware ceramic decorative art would have been fashioned simply because certain accomplished potters had been unable to resist the need to manifest their artistic capabilities. All these admirable artefacts were purposefully produced either in the hope of satisfying the fashionable desires of rich individual patrons or in response to the perceived demands of more widespread general markets. It was these wider markets which provided the opportunity and resource for the development of a large scale ceramic enterprise, and the successful anticipation of the character of the general market was as much the essential prerequisite for success in a large business then as it is today.

Chetham & Woolley's introduction of the new feldspathic stoneware body to their market could not have been better timed. The socio-economic conditions at the end of the eighteenth century had led to the creation of an enhanced requirement for good quality decorative artefacts in many materials including ceramics.

By the closing decades of the eighteenth century the Staffordshire pottery industry was growing strongly.[1] It was an element in the widespread advance of activity which was being experienced by so many sectors of the British economy at this time. This was a period of dramatic social and political change throughout Europe, and the economic consequence in Britain was, in a sense, the practical manifestation of a much longer episode of intellectual and cultural development usually referred to as the Enlightenment.[2] The main principle of this movement was the examination of the natural world and the structures of society through critical objective enquiry. The search for rational understanding, which had become the dominant and penetrating feature of intellectual progress in many European countries, was of long lineage.[3] In Britain early expression of such analytical enquiry can be traced from the late sixteenth and early seventeenth century pioneering works of Sir Francis Bacon,[4] through the unparalleled revelations in mathematics and physics of Sir Isaac Newton, and on to the powerful enquiries of the great British empirical philosophers, Locke, Berkeley and Hume, whose concepts deeply influenced European thought.[5]

The force of empirical enquiry had different consequences in different countries. In France, for example, the analytical questioning of the inequalities of the existing social and political order by powerful thinkers such as Rousseau and Voltaire (who acknowledged Francis Bacon's formative influence) was a contributing factor in the shift of social sentiment which culminated in the disorders of the Revolution of 1789. In Britain, certain alternative avenues of rational enquiry stimulated a different form of revolution, but it was still one which dramatically transformed the condition of the country's rapidly growing population.[6] With the aid of such bodies as the Society for the Encouragement of Arts, Manufactures and Commerce in London and, most importantly, the Lunar Society in the Midlands,[7] empirical analysis found expression amongst practical men who devised and delivered improvements in manufacturing processes and in agriculture.

Industrial productivity progressed at an accelerating pace from 1783 onwards, following the introduction of the Boulton and Watt rotary motion steam engines. These engines were capable of turning machinery and so motive power became available wherever needed; machine assisted manufacturing was no longer restricted to sites by rivers where water wheels could be installed or to breezy locations for windmills. In the second half of the eighteenth century there were also changes in agriculture. Land was more intensively enclosed and farming on a larger scale improved productivity with consequent financial benefits to the fewer farmers involved.[8]

The most obvious social effects of land enclosure and the growth of manufacturing in Britain were a progressive transition from rural to urban employment, and a consequent enlargement of cities and towns where industrial capital was concentrated.[9] A dramatic expansion of the country's wealth was a consequence of increased industry and commerce. A whole new class of rich and well-to-do individuals came into existence[10] and the first expression appeared of those imperatives which have formed the modern industrial world and consumer society.[11] Industry began to operate on a mass production scale, meeting the requirement for necessities and providing decorative artefacts, such as ceramics, for large and diverse groups of consumers. The demand for luxury items amongst the newly enriched has come to be regarded as an important spur to the wider economic changes of the period.[12]

An illustration of the impact these changes made on people living at the time can be found in a passage from the *Edinburgh Review* of 1813:

> In the whole history of the species, there was nothing at all comparable to the improvement of England within the last century. Never anywhere was there such an increase in wealth and luxury – so many admirable inventions in the arts – so many works of learning and ingenuity – such progress in cultivation – such an enlargement of commerce.

In the cultural sphere the disciplines of measured analysis which characterised empirical enquiry appear to be reflected in the popularity of the more ordered patterns of neo-classical design. Enthusiasm for classical ideas had been nurtured by the long dominance of Rome as the centre of artistic endeavour.[13] This was an era when many artists studied in Rome for a time and a European gentleman's education was scarcely complete without a visit to the Eternal City to absorb the influence of its buildings, classical ruins, paintings, and statues.

Many books were published with antique classical themes. Between 1719 and 1724 the Benedictine monk Bernard de Montfaucon produced *L'antiquite expliquee et representee en figures* which included an engraving of the Barberini Vase, a famous Roman glass masterpiece subsequently acquired from Sir William Hamilton by Margaret Cavendish-Harley, widow of the second Duke of Portland. Publications appearing later include Cochin and Bellicard's *Observations on the Antiquities of Herculaneum*, published in Paris in 1754, Stuart and Revett's *Antiquities of Athens*, published in London in 1762, and the magnificently illustrated account of Sir William Hamilton's collection of Greek and Roman vases, published by D'Hancarville in the years 1776 and 1777. There were many other such volumes.

In England, neo-classical taste was embraced and exploited by many of the new entrepreneurs of the Industrial Revolution. The principles of the division of labour, the powerful effects of which were explored in Adam Smith's famous work *The Wealth of Nations* (published in 1776), had previously been applied in the form of specialisation of task by the pioneers of industrial improvement. Matthew Boulton in the Birmingham metal trades at the Soho works and then Josiah Wedgwood, at Etruria in the Potteries were two of many businessmen who transformed what had been almost cottage enterprises into heavily capitalised productive factory-based industries.

With the development of specialised tasks, which was a basic principle of the factory phenomenon, came a sharper delineation between making and designing. Specialist industrial designers were required to help perfect artefacts for large quantity production. The pottery industry is a rich source of information about the workings of these new influences that were affecting many industries.

The records of the Wedgwood and Bentley partnership's library, prepared in August 1770, reveal that they owned most of the important works dealing with classical art forms.[14] The auction sale of the eminent Turner family's library in May 1813 also lists an important collection of primary reference works.[15] It is clear that sophisticated ceramic manufacturers such as Wedgwood and Turner were powerful disseminators of neo-classical taste. In their libraries they had wide sources of design material, they could afford to employ artists to search for new ideas[16] and modellers to adapt these ideas to manufacturing needs.[17] In their factories they reproduced the chosen designs in mass quantities and then distributed them through established marketing channels.[18]

Neo-classical designs were not the only popular patterns. Jugs and mugs in the unique fine honey coloured dry-bodied stoneware produced by the Turner family at their Lane End factory were often decorated with sprig relief compositions depicting domestic, tavern and rural life, together with country sports scenes, such as hunting, coursing and shooting.[19] The latter themes were perhaps popular amongst those who had prospered in agriculture or whose families had moved from the countryside to the towns.

The spirit of invention and enterprise in the latter decades of the eighteenth century enabled those who succeeded in their ventures to amass substantial personal fortunes. Scarcely ever before had the opportunities for financial advancement been so numerous. And those who did acquire fortunes also created a demand for other services associated with monetary wealth; professional practitioners such as lawyers, bankers, insurers, land agents and surveyors were in greater demand. At the same time there was a greater requirement for skilled workmen such as engineers and mechanics to make, install and maintain the machinery in the new factories. The relatively comfortable circumstances of this enlarged well-to-do element in the population created a bigger market for good quality decorative artefacts. In the past, fine decorative wares had been an unattainably expensive luxury, a trade patronised by a narrow, rich elite of the aristocracy, the gentry and the Church. As wealth spread more widely through the community, so the demand for 'luxury' wares arose amongst a less distinguished but more numerous clientele. Opportunities materialised for the new more productive factories to satisfy this broader demand with decorative artefacts manufactured on a larger scale.

In 1769 Josiah Wedgwood had moved production of his decorative wares into a new factory at Etruria in Stoke.[20] As the new patterns of demand developed, and perhaps as Etruria's productive capacity was itself increasing, Wedgwood began to adjust his business plans accordingly. He had established a large manufacturing unit and it needed to be fed with work. He was amongst the first to recognise that a manufacturer of luxury decorative wares could no longer afford to ignore the affluent non-aristocratic market which was being created by those who prospered in the new environment of enterprise. He wrote a letter about these changes to his business partner, Thomas Bentley, in August 1772:

> The Great People have had these vases in their Palaces long enough for them to be seen and admired by the Middling Class of people, which Class we know are greatly superior in number to the Great, and though a great price was at first necessary to make these vases esteemed 'Ornaments for Palaces' that reason no longer exists. Their character is established and the middling people would probably buy quantities of them at a reduced price...[21]

Josiah Wedgwood died in 1795. By then the 'Middling Class' were more numerous and the demand for good quality decorative artefacts had thereby also increased. By the close of the century there were many new large scale pottery factories capable of serving this 'Middling Class' market.[22] The innovative semi-translucent 'porcellaneous' feldspathic stoneware became a stylish new element within this trade. Although the Wedgwood factory had played such a pivotal role in the development of most forms of decorative dry-bodied stoneware, another business was first into the market with what became an important new product. In this instance the first rewards of innovation fell to Messrs. Chetham & Woolley of Lane End.

3.

THE DOCUMENTARY RECORD OF
CHETHAM & WOOLLEY

Until recently the Chetham & Woolley factory has received virtually no attention. The firm's name is only rarely mentioned in books dealing with English ceramics. No factory records have survived and no more than about a dozen marked pieces of the factory's wares are known at present. However, fortunately there is a small body of written evidence concerning the business which has survived. Though limited in scale, these documents indicate that from about 1795 to at least 1820 the company occupied an important position within the Staffordshire ceramic industry, and was particularly influential in relation to feldspathic stoneware.

One of the most discussed sources of information about the eighteenth century Staffordshire pottery industry was provided by a local inhabitant called Simeon Shaw. Although he was born in Salford, Lancashire sometime between 1784 and 1786, Shaw spent most of his life in the Staffordshire pottery towns. From 1818 to 1851 he was the principal of an academy for young gentlemen, first in Hanley and later at Tunstall.[1] Perhaps as a result of contacts made through this occupation it appears he became acquainted with some of the leading local manufacturers of his day. He assembled much information and wrote a now famous account of the early Staffordshire pottery industry in a book

dedicated to the renowned potter Josiah Spode.

The book of Simeon Shaw's studies is entitled *The History of the Staffordshire Potteries*. It was published in 1829, just over thirty years after the first appearance in the market of feldspathic stoneware. From his description of the characteristics of the material, it is clear that Simeon Shaw identified Chetham & Woolley as the inventors of this new type of dry-bodied stoneware. Towards the end of his book is the following passage:

About 1795, a new kind of pottery, a dry body, or without glaze or smear, was introduced into the market by Messrs. Chetham & Woolley, of Lane End. It is to the white pottery what jasper is to the coloured. Not being affected by change of temperature, but very fine in grain, durable in quality and of a most beautiful and delicate whiteness, it received the name it still bears, of Pearl, from Mr. J. Spode, at that time resident in London. It is used, like jasper, for the finest description of ornaments: and is in general estimation amongst all rank of society. Very few of the many attempts to produce pearl of equal excellence to the inventors, have been attended with any success...[2]

This is a most important paragraph. It followed a passage describing the unique honey-coloured stoneware of the John Turner factory and suggests that the Chetham & Woolley invention was thought to be of a separately discernable quality; an increased whiteness appears as one of its notable features. It is interesting that, in Simeon Shaw's opinion, hardly any competitors succeeded in making a material that could match Chetham & Woolley's 'Pearl' body. Shaw also draws attention to the fact that Chetham & Woolley's stoneware was used 'for the finest description of ornaments'. As ornamental wares are generally kept more carefully than utilitarian items, it is not impossible that more examples of these Chetham & Woolley wares will have survived.[3]

The first published record of the Chetham & Woolley partnership comes from the trade directories of 1793 onwards.[4] There is another important mention of the company in 1807, when the *Staffordshire Advertiser* records the death of James Chetham on the 16 August, aged fifty-three.[5] His will has recently been discovered in the Litchfield records office, and in the pre-amble James Chetham is described as a 'Gentleman Potter'.[6] Such a description implies that he was something above the ordinary class of tradesman; possibly it indicates that he owned land. It is known that his son, Jonathan Lowe Chetham, did own land in the parish of Blurton near Trentham Hall and perhaps this was inherited from his father.[7]

James Chetham's will also divulges that he and Richard Woolley were brothers- in-law.[8] Ann Chetham, James's wife, was Richard Woolley's sister and this perhaps helps to explain why the existing partnership arrangements were not completely abandoned following James's death. Instead, Ann Chetham continued the business in partnership with Richard Woolley, apparently by simply taking James's place. This arrangement must have required Richard Woolley's consent

and the close family tie probably facilitated the outcome.

However the partnership between Ann Chetham and Richard Woolley survived for only two years; in November 1809 it was dissolved when Richard Woolley left to go into business on his own.[9] He took a lease of the nearby Turner family factory which had become vacant in July 1806 following the bankruptcy of the Turner brothers, who were continuing to run the business founded by their father.[10] Unfortunately Richard Woolley's independent business venture was not a success and he became bankrupt in March 1811 after a brief trading period of just one year and four months.[11]

Meanwhile Ann Chetham persevered on her own at the Commerce Street works until 1814, when she was joined by her son, Jonathan Lowe Chetham, then aged twenty-one.[12] In 1818 the firm's name was changed to Chetham & Son and it remained so until Ann's death in 1821.[13] The following year, Jonathan Chetham was joined by a new partner, John Robinson,[14] and the firm traded as Chetham & Robinson until 1834 when Robinson's son, Samuel, joined them. For the next six years the business was known as Chetham & Robinson & Son. Following John Robinson's death in 1840,[15] Samuel Robinson left the company and Jonathan Lowe Chetham traded as sole proprietor from 1841 until his death in 1861. His sons, John, Robert and Frederick then jointly took charge of the business, trading as J.R. & F. Chetham. The firm, then named Frederick Chetham & Co., eventually came to an end in 1871, apparently due to disagreement between the partners.[16]

Throughout its trading life under the various controlling interests, the enterprise operated from the Commerce Street premises and members of the Chetham family were continuously active within the firm during its lifetime. In light of the events mentioned in the previous paragraphs, the title Chetham & Woolley can only strictly be applied to the period from c.1793 until Richard Woolley's departure from the business in November 1809. Some of the pieces to be examined in this book will have been made at the time when Ann Chetham was managing the company alone (1809-1814) or in the later period when she had the assistance of her son, Jonathan Lowe. Therefore, these pieces might more accurately be termed 'Chetham'. Unfortunately nearly all the articles made by the factory are unmarked so it is not easy to date items with precision. There are a few exceptions, where pieces are impress marked 'CHETHAM & WOOLLEY', 'CHETHAM', or where they carry a date. The pieces examined in the following sections were all made in the Commerce Street factory originally styled Chetham & Woolley and it therefore seems most straightforward to bring them all under this title.

Even after Richard Woolley's departure the combined names of Chetham & Woolley preserved an identity beyond the dissolution of the original partnership. Sometime after the failure of Woolley's independent business in 1811 he gave the formula for the new pearl stoneware to a local potter called John Riley. The brothers John and Richard Riley were well-respected partners of a pottery business in Burslem from 1796 to 1828. They maintained a book of formulae which has survived and is now preserved in the Potteries Museum Archive at Hanley. The following entry was made by John Riley:

Pearl Body
The first made by Messrs. Chetham & Woolley and made by them for several years in teapots, Morters, Jugs, etc. Mr. Woolley gave it to the writer Jno. Riley after he had given over business.

3. Composition ground
1. Blue Clay, or Brownish Blue Clay
To be placed in glost saggars, washed every time they are used in the biscuit oven, with cream colour glaze. This is the best wash. One side towards the saggar that is glazed. The other side of the ware must have a glost bat to it, made the shape of the ware, and first glazed every time.[17]

This is a helpful record and it provides information about the wares that Chetham & Woolley were producing from the feldspathic stoneware formula; it also confirms that they made the wares over a long period of time. The Riley brothers were substantial figures in the pottery industry of their day and John Riley would have been unlikely to have recorded a formula he thought of no importance. The interest in feldspar is also evident from another passage in the Riley book which gives a description of the various types of clay.[18]

Where the Chetham & Woolley business is mentioned in contemporary trade directories it is listed as making 'Egyptian Black, Pearl, and Earthenware in General'.[19] The firm's name also appears in the records of an important London dealer in Staffordshire ware called Thomas Wyllie.[20] These records reveal that Wyllie purchased a substantial proportion of his stock from Chetham & Woolley in the years between 1794 and 1799. Sadly no account is given of the types of ware the company was selling to Wyllie – they may have been sending him 'Egyptian Black or Earthenware in General' rather than 'Pearl' – but it is clear that by the close of the eighteenth century Chetham & Woolley were trading on such a scale that they could satisfy a large proportion of the requirements of a substantial London dealer.

Another important reference to Chetham &

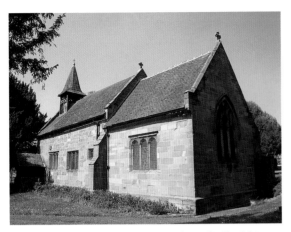

Plate 1. Blurton Church, near Trentham, Staffordshire.

Plate 2. Wall tiles in Blurton Church.

Plate 3. Wall tile recording Jonathan Lowe Chetham (James Chetham's son).

Woolley comes in a discussion concerning the invention of Parian Ware which was conducted through newspaper correspondence in the *Staffordshire Advertiser* during September 1851. One of the letters claims that Parian Ware was only a modified version of the 'pearl' body invented by Chetham & Woolley over sixty years earlier.[21]

Later, there is a clear testimony to the importance that the Chetham family attained within their local community in the existence of a series of wall tiles in St. Bartholemew's Church, Blurton, on the road between the Staffordshire towns of Trentham and Longton (Plate 1).[22] These tiles record the names of prominent past parishioners. They include Jonathan Lowe Chetham, his wife Elizabeth, and also his daughter and son-in-law (Plate 3). It is not unreasonable to infer that the Chetham pottery business itself was of local importance.

There is therefore a small but useful body of documentary evidence concerning Chetham & Woolley. It all suggests that in the late eighteenth and early ninetheenth centuries the Chetham & Woolley Commerce Street enterprise was a substantial concern. We know the firm was capable of satisfying the requirements of one substantial London customer, Thomas Wyllie, and there may well have been others. The invention by the partnership of an important new product for the Staffordshire industry, the 'pearl', suggests a considerable level of technical expertise and it is also clear from Simeon Shaw's records that pearl was used 'for the finest description of ornaments' and was unmatched in excellence.

It would be surprising if no examples of pearl stonewares had survived from such an apparently important factory. Fortunately many pieces have survived, as will be shown in the following sections. The wares discovered so far support the contention that Chetham & Woolley made wares of a quality and elegance in both form and decoration which was equalled by few other contemporary factories.

4.

THE OAK-LEAF BORDER GROUP

In 1962 the Staffordshire Potteries Museum acquired a large black basalt stoneware teapot (Plate 4).[1] The quality of this piece is of a high order. The body has a smooth, dense consistency, the engine turning at the lower section of the main form is complex and well executed, and the sprig relief decoration is crisp and clear. The teapot has a number of noteworthy features.

First, the cover is topped with a finial which, although broken, has sufficient of the moulded model remaining to identify a well known composition of Venus with Cupid. Venus is seated and clasps Cupid to her bosom. Cupid holds a small arrow of love against his mother's breast.[2]

A second and most important feature appears at the junction of the teapot's shoulder with the main body. Here a distinctive moulded oak-leaf border band runs all the way round the piece. Border motifs of oak and laurel leaves or geometric patterns at this position on teapots are commonly found amongst the wares of several makers of the period. For example, teapots made by Wedgwood, Turner, Adams, Neale, Birch and Greenwood all carry similar features.[3] However, the detail of the patterns used by these various makers differs in each case. Most factories had their own special pattern, and this seems to be the

case for the border on this large basalt teapot as well.

Most importantly there can be no doubt about which factory made the teapot because in the clay of the base are the words 'Chetham & Woolley, Lane End – RW' (Plate 5). The script is handwritten and would have been done at the point when the material was in the 'leather hard' state prior to firing (see Appendix 3a). It is not particularly surprising that Chetham and Woolley should have made a black basalt teapot because, as mentioned above, local trade directories included Egyptian Black (basalt) amongst their range of products.

The date '1775' is written on the base, but it has been scratched out of the finished base after firing. The date is unquestionably a spurious later addition and was presumably an attempt to make the piece appear older than it is.

In the 1970s a partial redevelopment of the Lane End area of Longton, was undertaken and in the process some buildings in Chancery Lane, close to the Chetham & Woolley factory site, were demolished. An enterprising member of public took the opportunity to look for shards in the cleared spaces and several interesting example were found. Subsequent enquiries have established that all the shards were discovered in the soil of footings under a demolished Chancery

Plate 4. Large basalt teapot, height: 21cm, 1795-1800.
CITY MUSEUM AND ART GALLERY, STOKE

Plate 5. 'Chetham & Woolley Lane End – RW' written in a script hand into the base of the teapot (Plate 4).

Lane building which had once been part of a Victorian factory belonging to the Locketts, a family of potters.[4] Before the Lockett factory was built, this land adjacent to the existing Chetham and Woolley factory may have been an open area suitable for dumping. The shards were all found as a group in the same soil level. Amongst the group

was the basalt stoneware fragment shown in Plate 6. The shards are now preserved in the Potteries Museum and Art Gallery, Stoke-on-Trent.

The shard in Plate 6 is clearly part of a handle and on the inner surface there are traces of an oak-leaf border pattern. The details of this feature conform precisely to those of the oak-leaf border

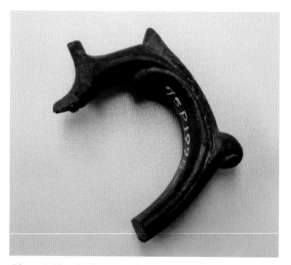

*Plate 6. Shard of pottery found close to the Chetham &
Woolley factory.* CITY MUSEUM AND ART GALLERY, STOKE

*Plate 7. A fragment of the oak-leaf border feature on a
shard which has a matching border to a Chetham &
Woolley teapot.*

running round the shoulder of the large basalt
teapot (Plate 4). This precise border pattern is not
found on any known wares from other makers of
the period. The implication, therefore, is that the
shard also originally came from an item of basalt
stoneware made by Chetham & Woolley. The
correspondence between the oak-leaf features on
the shard and the marked basalt teapot can be
seen clearly in Plate 7.

It is not unreasonable to surmise that the other
shards from this deposit might also have
originally belonged to wares made by Chetham
and Woolley. Another black basalt fragment
found in the group is shown in Plate 8. It has the
distinctive features of a flat angled surface
leading to a scalloped gallery.

A combination of the same distinctive features
as found on the shard is also found on a
feldspathic dry-bodied stoneware teapot illustrated in Plate 9. Here too the flat angled surface
on the shoulder leads to a similarly scalloped

*Plate 8. Basalt shard from the group found nearby the
Chetham & Woolley Commerce Street site. Width approx.
8cm.* CITY MUSEUM AND ART GALLERY, STOKE

gallery. It also has a prominent oak-leaf border
feature running round the main body at the
junction with the shoulder. The details of this
border correspond exactly with the oak-leaf
border which apppears in the same position on
the Chetham & Woolley basalt teapot (Plate 4).
As shown in Plate 10, the teapot also has a cover

Plate 9. A feldspathic dry-bodied stoneware teapot with the same features as the basalt shard, unmarked, 1795-1805.
PRIVATE COLLECTION

Plate 10. A feldspathic teapot. Height 16cm. Unmarked 1795-1805.
PRIVATE COLLECTION

Plate 11. The lid of the teapot in Plate 10 showing Venus and Cupid finial.

Plate 12. Oak-leaf border teapot with straight spout and simple handle. 1795-1805. Present location unknown (previously in the Bentley Collection).

with the Venus and Cupid finial (see Plate 11). This again matches the broken finial on the cover of the marked basalt teapot (Plate 4).

The correspondence of the oak-leaf border and the other features of the feldspathic dry-bodied stoneware teapot with the teapot shown in Plate 4 and the shard in Plate 8 leads to the reasonable conclusion that they were all made by the Chetham & Woolley partnership. The teapot shown in Plate 11 appears to be a surviving example of the factory's 'pearl' stoneware.

The search in recent years for other items of Chetham & Woolley 'pearl' stoneware with the special oak-leaf border feature has established that the teapot shown in Plate 10 is by no means the only surviving example. Many similar

Plates 13a and 13b. Chetham & Woolley Venus and Cupid finials showing the two different styles in which Venus's hair falls.
PRIVATE COLLECTION

Plate 14. Oak-leaf border teapot with acorn finial. Height 13cm. Unmarked. 1795-1805. PRIVATE COLLECTION

feldspathic dry-bodied stoneware oak-leaf border teapots have been located in the collections of museums and private individuals in both the UK and the USA. Whilst similar in all important respects, including the identifying features and the texture of the body, they are not all in exactly the same form. The teapot in Plate 10 has a curved spout and a spurred handle, whilst other examples have straight spouts or simpler handles in various combinations. An example of one such combination is shown in Plate 12. Different permutations of product design within the grouping are to be expected in cases where items were in

production for several years as this would have provided a cost effective way of catering for a variety of tastes within a uniform product pattern.

A feature which is useful in identifying the oak-leaf border wares is found in association with the cover finials such as the Venus and Cupid shown in Plate 11. The finial is surrounded by a border composed of large leaves with smaller ones in between and this precise form commonly appears on Chetham & Woolley wares of this group. Although not always present, it is a supporting aid to attribution in cases where it does appear. Again, as with the oak-leaf border

Plate 15. Oak-leaf border teapot with Widow of Zarephath finial. Height 15cm. 1795-1805. Location unknown

itself, care must be taken to identify that the exact form matches this particular finial 'leaf surround' feature because similar borders were used by other stoneware manufacturers of the period.

Care must also be taken with pieces which portray the Venus and Cupid finial. This feature alone is not sufficient to identify a Chetham & Woolley piece; at least one other contemporary maker, Samuel Hollins, used an almost identical finial moulding.[5] However, Samuel Hollins stoneware appears almost universally to have been made in dry-bodied material of an unusual colouring – buff, sage green or brown – very delicately and

crisply sprig decorated and sometimes highlighted with carefully applied coloured enamelling. None has been discovered so far that has been made from 'pearl' feldspathic dry-bodied stoneware of the of the Chetham & Woolley type.

It was once suggested that the way to tell the difference between the Venus and Cupid finials of a Chetham & Woolley item from those of a Samuel Hollins piece is by the style of the hair at the back of Venus's head because in all of the examples produced by the latter the hair falls straight down rather than to one side.[6] Although this was a perfectly reasonable proposition when

Plate 16. Coffee pot with oak-leaf border. Height 49cm. c.1800. Unmarked.

VICTORIA AND ALBERT MUSEUM, LONDON

Plates 17 and 18. Two oak-leaf border coffee pots with unusual finials, c.1800. Height and location not known.

first presented, it did not unfortunately survive the test of subsequent discoveries – the Chetham & Woolley Venus and Cupid finials in Plates 13a and 13b show the hair falling straight down in one case and to the side in the other.

Venus and Cupid finials were not the only ones to appear on Chetham & Woolley wares. The teapots illustrated in Plates 14 and 15 share the same 'pearl' body and all the other typical features of the factory's oak-leaf border group. However, in these examples one has a simple acorn knop (Plate 14) and the other (Plate 15) a representation

Plate 19. Chetham & Woolley coffee pot, but lacking the oak-leaf border. Unmarked, c.1800. Height 45cm.
WARRINGTON MUSEUM

31

Plate 20. Oak-leaf border helmet shaped creamer, c.1800. Height 11.5cm

of the Widow of Zarephath, a well known and popular finial moulding of the period.[7]

A common decoration on the oak-leaf border teapots illustrated above is blue enamel edging and banding which outlines features such as the handles or scalloped galleries, or places emphasis elsewhere. This was a widely employed decorative technique and Plate 15 shows how additional enamel decoration in green and blue has been applied to the leafy border surrounding the Widow of Zeraphath. The simple but effective enhancement of the basics designs with enamel edging and banding is frequently found, but examples with additional enamelling are rare. In

Plate 21. Oak-leaf border sucrier, c.1800. Height 14cm.
PRIVATE COLLECTION
Plate 22. Sucrier, c.1800. Height 9cm. Unmarked.
PRIVATE COLLECTION
Plate 23. Sucrier, c.1800. Height 8.5cm. Unmarked.
PRIVATE COLLECTION

several known examples the finished dry-bodied 'pearl' stoneware has been left entirely untouched without enamel decoration of any kind.

Teapots are not the only category of feldspathic dry-bodied stonewares within the Chetham & Woolley oak-leaf border group. Elegant coffee pots also display the identifying features of the grouping, as illustrated in Plate 16. Recent research has again unearthed many similar oak-leaf border feldspathic stoneware coffee pots in various collections in the UK and USA. Nearly all the examples discovered so far have either the Venus and Cupid or the Widow of Zarephath finial, more commonly the former. However there are one or two exceptions, as shown below in Plates 17 and 18, but coffee pots with finials such as these are extremely rare.[8]

Virtually all Chetham & Woolley pearl dry-bodied stoneware oak-leaf border coffee pots are finished with an easily identifiable complex handle comprising a double 'C' scroll and spur joined to the upper body by a short horizontal bar. This particular design of handle appears to be a special feature of the factory's coffee pots and may be regarded as a powerful indicator for attribution. Again, as in the case of the Chetham & Woolley teapots, there are variations between

Plate 24. Oak-leaf border bowl. c.1800. Height 9cm, Diameter 20.5cm. Unmarked.   PRIVATE COLLECTION

coffee pots, but they still all conform to a generally uniform product pattern. The coffee pot illustrated in Plate 19 has nearly all the identifying features of the oak-leaf border group.

As well as being made from the characteristic 'pearl' body, this coffee pot has a Venus and Cupid finial surrounded by the associated leafy border, with the larger leaves picked out in green enamel. In addition there is the characteristc double 'C' scroll and spur handle. However, this coffee pot lacks a moulded oak-leaf border and has a thin blue enamel band instead. Despite this, and given the presence of all the other characteristic features, feldspathic dry-bodied stoneware coffee pots such as this may reasonably be attributed to the Chetham & Woolley product range. As was noted in the case

Plate 25. Oak-leaf border covered jug, c.1800.

NEWARK MUSEUM, NJ

of the teapots, where a maker was active over a long period of time, attempts would have been made to stimulate untapped demand in the most economic way by creating relatively minor variants around a standard form, much as manufacturers of consumer goods do today.

Ancillary vessels to accompany teapots and coffee pots are also found within the Chetham & Woolley oak-leaf border range. A small helmet shaped oak-leaf border cream jug is shown in Plate 20, and Plate 21 is a circular sucrier.

The sucrier in Plate 21 is particularly noteworthy in that it has a Venus and Cupid finial within the associated leafy surround, the same features as have been illustrated previously on the teapots (Plate 11) and coffee pots (Plate 16). Other types of Chetham & Woolley oak-leaf border feldspathic stoneware sucriers are also known as shown in Plates 22 and 23.

Other items within the oak-leaf border group include bowls (Plate 24), a covered jug (Plate 25) and a large metal handled kettle (Plate 26).

The covered jug in Plate 25 again has the typical features of a Venus and Cupid finial within the characteristic leafy surround, in this case enamelled in green and blue. The sprig relief decoration on the kettle in Plate 26 is also particularly interesting. A group of four figures is portrayed: a male and a female figure represent the Shakespearean characters of MacBeth and Lady MacBeth, a third female figure represents Britannia carrying the royal crown on a cushion, and fourth female figure is France, bound in chains with a crown pierced with a dagger at her feet.

The allegory can be deciphered as follows: whilst Britain's monarchy was secure, the King of France, Louis XVI, had been executed by order of the revolutionary courts on 21 January, 1793. Hence, the Macbeth's are included as regicides and the crown is pieced with a dagger at

Plate 26. Large oak-leaf border kettle with rafia bound metal handle, c.1800. Height 25.5cm. Unmarked.

PRIVATE COLLECTION

the feet of the female figure representing France.

In light of this, the piece must have been made after Louis XVI had been killed. However, in 1802 Britain signed the short-lived Peace of Amiens and a message clearly condemning the regicide would then have been rendered unsuitable for the market. Nor would it have been particularly suitable after the collapse of the peace in 1803, since that was a full decade after the execution. Therefore it seems most likely the kettle was made between the years 1793 and 1802.

Interestingly another element of the sprig relief decoration on the kettle is of the goddess Cybele. Precisely the same moulding is found on the marked Chetham & Woolley black basalt teapot described at the beginning of this section.

5.

'PEARL' STONEWARE JUGS

Chetham & Woolley made an extensive range of 'pearl' dry-bodied stoneware jugs. The great majority have a pronounced spiral on the upper surface of the interior base which indicates that they were thrown on a potter's wheel. The exterior would then have been shaped by appropriate templates and tools whilst turning either on a lathe or potter's wheel. In nearly all cases the lower part of the feldspathic stoneware jugs were engine turned above the base before firing (see Appendix 3). Almost all Chetham & Woolley 'pearl' stoneware jugs have sprig relief decoration and in a large number of cases it depicts a hunting scene.

Jugs decorated with sprig relief hunting scenes were particularly popular product for most stoneware manufacturers in the period from end of the eighteenth to the opening decades of the nineteenth centuries.[1] Many factories made them in large numbers and consequently they now are one of the most commonly found feldspathic stoneware objects. The 'pearl' feldspathic stoneware jugs made by Chetham & Woolley can be distinguished from the many surviving examples of other makers and a typical feldspathic dry-bodied stoneware hunting scene jug is shown in Plates 27-29 decorated with a pattern called 'The Kill'.

Feldspathic stoneware potters of the period appear to have used 'The Kill' more than any other hunting scene and it is almost always presented in precisely the same form and sequence.

When the jug handle is placed to the right, at the far right hand side of the scene stands a tall tree. To the left of the tree are tethered two saddled hunting horses without riders. To the left of the horses a huntsman stands at a wooden fence with foxhounds coming through and over it. Next, there is another huntsman climbing over the fence, helping himself up by his right arm which is hooked over the branch of a nearby bushy tree. Then there is a group of four foxhounds surrounding and dispatching a supine fox. Finally there is another tall tree arching towards the hounds.

Sprig relief pictures such as this were placed on the surface of a piece before it was fired (See Appendix 1). The relief effect was obtained by using shallow intaglio sprig moulds which were first filled with a stoneware body, either identical to or compatible with the surface composition of the main object. This material was pricked out of the intaglio mould, forming a small relief casting which was carefully applied to the surface of the object. The finished item, complete with sprig relief decoration, was then fired in one passage through the kiln.

Although the 'The Kill' appears as a unified composition, the complete picture was not

Plates 27, 28 and 29. Feldspathic dry-bodied stoneware jug, sprig decorated with a hunting scene called 'The Kill'. Unmarked, 1800-1810. Height 14cm.

applied in one continuous slab of clay. It was made up by using a number of separate small sprig moulds, each contributing a part of the whole scene. These sprig relief elements were then carefully joined together in situ on the surface of the item.

In the case of 'The Kill', for example, six sprig moulds were used to complete the picture: one for the hounds dispatching the fox, one for the tethered horses, two for the huntsmen, and one for each of the trees. Two of the sprigs from this picture are shown in Plates 30 and 31. The straight edges are where adjacent mouldings could be joined together without interrupting the flow of the scene.

Some sprig moulds from 'The Kill' were also used for other scenes. For example, the trees at the beginning and end of the sequence, one of which is shown in Plate 30, are often found in pictures entirely unrelated to hunting. It is also interesting to note that popular sprig relief pictures such as 'The Kill' are often found in

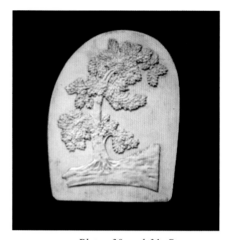
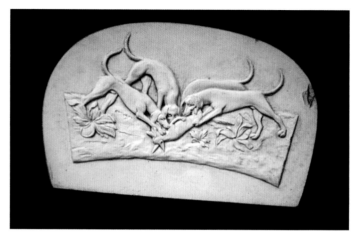

Plates 30 and 31. Stoneware sprig relief casts from which intaglio sprig moulds would be taken.   SPODE MUSEUM TRUST

exactly the same form on the feldspathic stoneware products of several different makers. For example the relief scene appears on all three mugs shown in Plate 32.

Although these mugs were all made between 1800 and 1815, they have little in common other than the same hunting scene – the handles, proportions and body textures are all different. Also, the lower portions of these mugs have different engine turned decorative treatments, a widely used finishing technique for stonewares of this period (see Appendix 3). These differences make it unlikely that the mugs were made by the same factory despite the use of 'The Kill' in apparently identical forms. Fortunately the three mugs are marked, so there is no question about where they were made. They were produced, from right to left, by Elijah Mayer, Job Ridgway and Davenport.

The three jugs illustrated in Plate 33 also all have the same hunting picture, but in this case it is an unusual one and rare in comparison to 'The Kill'. As well as the hunting pattern being the same, there are other similarities between the jugs.

The body texture is the same and has a pronounced orange coloured translucency. The handles are also the same, as are the overall proportions despite the differences in size. They each have the same brown colouring at the neck and shoulder, and the engine turned decoration of the lower sections is also the same. These common attributes would be strongly persuasive that the jugs had all been made by the same factory even if there was no other evidence. Fortunately again all the jugs are impress marked so there is no doubt that all three were made by T. & J. Hollins.

Another interesting group of three feldspathic stoneware jugs is shown in Plate 34. Each is sprig relief decorated with the same but very unusual hunting scene. These jugs are not marked, but they do all have many features in common. They are all made from the same feldspathic dry-bodied stoneware and share an identical texture and translucency. The overall proportions are the same in every case and they all have the same form of moulded beak, as well as the same unusual handles, examples of which are shown in Plate 35.

Plate 32. Three feldspathic stoneware mugs each sprig relief decorated with 'The Kill'. Impress marked (right to left): E. Mayer, J. Ridgway, and Davenport. 1800-1815. Height: 11.5cm, 10cm and 8.5cm respectively. PRIVATE COLLECTION

Plate 33. Three feldspathic stoneware jugs, each with sprig relief decorations of an unusual hunting pattern. All are impress marked T. & J. Hollins. 1800-1810. Heights: 22cm, 18cm, and 16cm. PRIVATE COLLECTION

In addition to having identical distinctive handles and moulded beaks, these jugs all have the same and the engine turned decoration, which in each case is composed of sixty-four uniform and equally spaced vertical ridges. Most impor-tantly, all the jugs in Plate 34 have the same sprig relief decoration of the unusual hunting scene. Indeed, this scene has not been found on any jugs which do not share the other common features of this particular class of jugs.

Plate 34. Three feldspathic dry-bodied stoneware jugs each sprig relief decorated with the same rare hunting pattern. Unmarked. 1795-1810. Heights: 23cm, 20cm, 17cm.

PRIVATE COLLECTION

Another pair of feldspathic dry-bodied stoneware sprig decorated hunting jugs is shown in Plate 36. Both jugs have much in common with the group of three shown in Plate 34. They share the same body texture and translucency, their overall proportions are the same, and they have the unusual handles shown in Plate 35. The moulded beaks are also the same, as is the engine turning decoration. However, there is one important difference – the hunting scene on the two jugs in Plate 36, though equally unusual, is not the same as that on those in Plate 34.

Closer examination reveals a most interesting feature which is common to the jugs in Plate 36

Plate 35. Distinctive handles found on feldspathic dry-bodied stoneware jugs of the type illustrated in Plate 34.

Plate 36. Two feldspathic dry-bodied stoneware jugs each sprig relief decorated with a rare hunting pattern. Unmarked. 1795-1810. Heights; 23cm & 16cm.

PRIVATE COLLECTION

Plate 37. Final feature of rare sprig relief decorated hunting scene on all five feldspathic dry-bodied stoneware jugs in Plates 34 and 36.

and also the previous group of three in Plate 34. If the sprig relief decoration on both these sets of jugs is analysed in terms of the separate moulds used to compose their very unusual hunt scenes, it becomes clear that the final part of the scene – the last sprig mould – is the same on all of the jugs. On the three jugs in Plate 34 the earlier elements of the sprig relief hunting scene are different from those on the jugs in Plate 36, but the scene on all five jugs is finished with the same view of an escaping fox (see Plate 37).

Further analysis of the sprig relief hunting

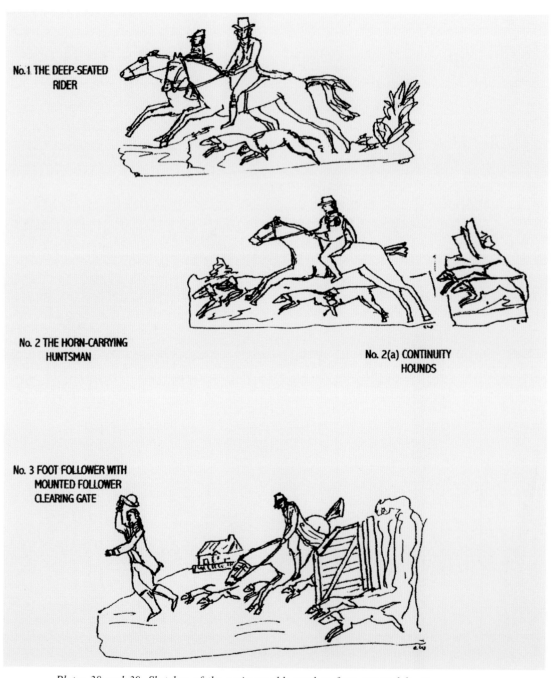

No. 1. THE DEEP-SEATED
RIDER

No. 2 THE HORN-CARRYING
HUNTSMAN

No. 2(a) CONTINUITY
HOUNDS

No. 3 FOOT FOLLOWER WITH
MOUNTED FOLLOWER
CLEARING GATE

Plates 38 and 39. Sketches of the sprig moulds used to form unusual hunting scenes on feldspathic dry-bodied stoneware jugs in Plates 34 and 36. C. WYMAN

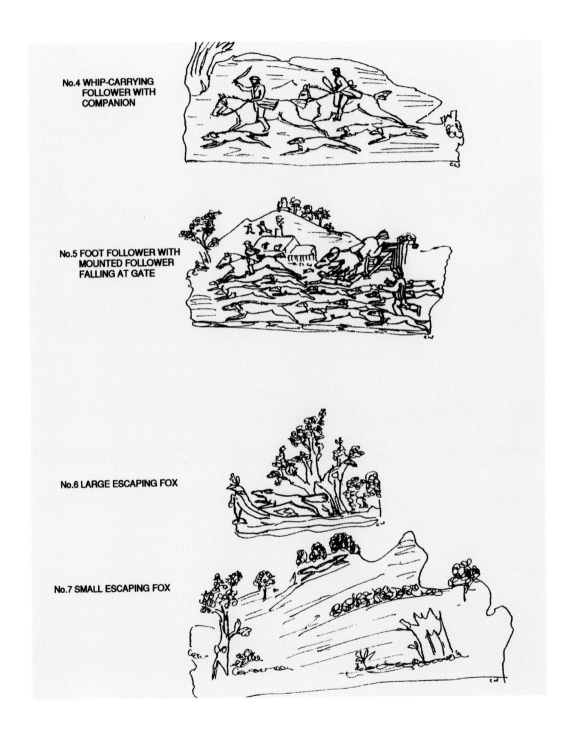

No.4 WHIP-CARRYING
FOLLOWER WITH
COMPANION

No.5 FOOT FOLLOWER WITH
MOUNTED FOLLOWER
FALLING AT GATE

No.6 LARGE ESCAPING FOX

No.7 SMALL ESCAPING FOX

scenes on all five jugs in Plates 34 and 36 discloses that the two apparently different pictures can all be composed by combining different elements from a common pool of seven main sprig moulds and one subsidiary sprig mould. All of the sprig relief hunting scenes on all the jugs were composed in this way. These source sprig moulds are identified in Plates 38 and 39.

Plate 40. Feldspathic stone-ware sprig relief jug, impress marked 'CHETHAM & WOOLLEY'. 1795-1810, Height: 30.5cm.

PRIVATE COLLECTION, UK

Plate 41. Impressed mark at base of handle of jug in Plate 40.

Plate 42. Feldspathic dry-bodied stoneware jug, notable for the rectangular shaped handle. Unmarked. 1800-1810. Height: 16.5cm. PRIVATE COLLECTION

The titles given to the sprig moulds are as follows:

1   The deep-seated rider
2   The horn-carrying huntsman
2a   Continuity hounds (the subsidiary sprig)
3   Foot follower with mounted follower clearing gate
4   The whip-carrying follower and companion
5   Foot follower with mounted follower falling at gate
6   Large escaping fox
7   Small escaping fox

The hunting scenes on the jugs in Plate 34 were composed from sprig moulds 4, 5 and 6. Those in Plate 36 were created by drawing together sprig moulds 1, 2a, 3 and 6.

The reason for pursuing this analysis of sprig relief decorated hunting scenes lies in their connection to two other jugs, one in the USA (in the collection of the Colonial Williamsburg Foundation) and the other in the UK (in a private collection). The latter is illustrated in Plate 40.

This jug has many characteristics in common with the five unmarked jugs in Plates 34 and 36. It has the same feldspathic body in terms of

Plates 43 and 44. Feldspathic stoneware jug sprig relief decorated with a hunting scene. Unmarked. Dated 1804. Height: 16.5cm.   PRIVATE COLLECTION

texture and translucency, the same shape of handle, the same proportions, the same type of moulded beak and the same engine turning decoration. Most importantly, it has a sprig relief hunting scene composed of moulds from the pool of seven from which all of the pictures on the five unmarked jugs were made. The combination for the jug in Plate 40 is sprig moulds 1, 2a, 5 and 6. Significantly, this latter jug is also marked – impressed at the base of the handle are the names 'CHETHAM & WOOLLEY'.

The number of common features shared between the unmarked jugs and the marked Chetham & Woolley jug in Plate 40 makes it is reasonable to conclude that the five unmarked jugs in Plates 34 and 36 were also made by that factory. They are representative of typical Chetham & Woolley feldspathic dry-bodied stoneware jugs of which over forty examples – all unmarked – have

now been discovered and identified in various collections in both the UK and USA.

The identification of the group of seven factory associated sprig moulds in Plates 38 and 39 makes it possible to recognise another group of the Chetham & Woolley hunting scene jugs. The link is the jug in Plate 42 which is made from the same 'pearl' feldspathic stoneware body, with the same engine turned decoration to the lower section, and where the hunting scene is composed from some of the special Chetham & Woolley associated sprigs, in this case moulds 4, 5 and 7.

One difference between this and the other jugs is that the handle shape in this case is of a rectangular form. However, since the sprig moulds creating the hunting scene are so strongly associated with the Chetham & Woolley jugs examined previously, it leads to the reasonable deduction that the factory also made jugs with

Plate 45. Feldspathic stoneware jugs in the same Chetham & Woolley 'pearl' body, all with the same rectangular shaped handles. Unmarked 1800-1810. Heights: 17cm, 16.5cm and 10cm.   PRIVATE COLLECTION

Plate 46. Follower head first into stream.
Plate 47. Follower riding strongly with companion appearing.
Plate 48. Upright rider clearing gate.
Plate 49. Fox escaping amongst rocks.   C. WYMAN

these rectangular shaped handles. This makes it possible to identify another grouping of sprig relief decorated hunting scene jugs and another set of factory associated sprig moulds.

Plate 50. An unusual sprig relief moulded tavern scene on a Chetham & Woolley feldspathic dry-bodied stoneware jug. 1795-1810. Height: 21cm   PRIVATE COLLECTION

Plate 51. Three Chetham & Woolley feldspathic stoneware presentation jugs each with enamel decoration within an oval surround of a rural scene with the initial 'J. A' in puce enamel copper plate script and the date 1801 in black. Unmarked. Heights: 23.5cm, 20.5cm and 17.5cm.
PRIVATE COLLECTION

Plates 52 and 53. Chetham & Woolley feldspathic stoneware covered jug with vines and yellow banding, lined with maroon around neck. The handle and moulded beak are outlined in blue enamel and the main body enamel is painted with a rural landscape. The initials 'WSS' appear in purple script on the top of the handle. Unmarked. 1795-1805. Height: 25cm. NORTHAMPTON MUSEUM

The jug shown in Plates 43 and 44 also has the square handle and is a personalised piece with the name John Robotham beneath the beak, accompanied by the date 1804. It is made from the typical Chetham & Woolley 'pearl' feldspathic stoneware body. Many similar jugs of various different sizes are known and all have the same rectangular handle. A small representative group of these is shown in Plate 45.

Jugs of this grouping are commonly sprig relief decorated in a hunting scene composed of four sprig moulds, always appearing in the same sequence. They are shown and titled in that fixed sequence in Plates 46 to 49.

This group of sprig moulds provides a further aid for identifying Chetham & Woolley wares. A similar scene is occasionally found of the feldspathic stoneware of other makers, however, so care must be taken in examining the details of the sprig moulds, particularly the first in the sequence, Plate 46.

In the Chetham & Woolley sprig mould, the fallen follower appears to have gone head-first into the stream he is trying to cross. In the case of other makers the follower appears to land in the stream on his back, so that most of the torso is visible and not just the lower half. The Chetham & Woolley version of these sprig moulds also appear in the same sequence on other categories of the factory's output as will be shown later.

Not all of the Chetham & Woolley jugs are sprig decorated with hunting scenes. Rare examples are

Plate 54. Two Chetham & Wolley jugs, both sprig decorated with the same hunting scene. Unmarked. 1795-1810. Heights: 18cm, 20.5cm. PRIVATE COLLECTION

Plate 55. Slip moulded feldspathic stoneware jug, sprig decorated with unusual hunting scene composed of Chetham & Woolley factory associated sprig moulds. Sprig mould 1 is shown. Unmarked. 1800-1810. Height: 15cm. PRIVATE COLLECTION

known with tavern or rustic scenes. Plate 50, for example, shows the scene from one such jug which depicts a tavern party. This is an unusual adaptation of sprig relief decoration – a scene derived from a painting by David Teniers – which is often found on Turner and Herculaneum wares.[2]

Many Chetham & Woolley items became presentation or commemorative pieces, usually with the recipient's initials carefully written in a stylish copperplate script. The jugs illustrated in Plates 51-53 are fine examples of this category. They have all of the previously mentioned characteristics of the standard Chetham & Woolley hunting jugs, but there is no sprig relief decoration. All are dated 1801. Another exceptional presentation jug, this time with a cover and strainer behind the beak, is shown in Plates

52 and 53.

One presentation jug is known which is also decorated with a hunting scene made from the first group of factory associated sprig moulds in Plates 38 and 39. This presentation jug is seen in Plate 54 side by side with a standard hunting jug; sprig mould 4 from the first group of seven is shown on both.

Another variation sometimes found at the base of Chetham & Woolley jugs is in the extent of engine turned decoration. In some examples the turning that was applied was much finer. The result of this is that the number of vertical engine turned lines increases from sixty-four to one hundred and twenty. There are a few rare examples where engine turning of the base is entirely absent and the lower section above the base is left completely smooth.

It is not known whether the enamel decoration of Chetham & Woolley presentation wares was executed in house or by outside decorators. It is likely that simple border decorations may have been done in house, but even this is not certain. As for more developed compositions, such as those shown in Plate 51, it is possible that outside decorators did the work on behalf of the factory or perhaps bought undecorated wares to decorate and trade on their own account. The enamel palette of the more elaborately decorated presentation pieces such as Plate 53 is more complex and this may suggest external work. However, though colourful, the compositions are relatively naïve in structure and sentiment.

One intriguing possibility is that Richard Woolley himself may have been responsible for in house enamel decoration before he left the partnership in November 1809. In a letter to the Marquis of Stafford following his father's bankruptcy, Samuel Woolley, relates that his father had been to Milan in order to 'endeavour by orna-

(Left and Centre) *Plates 56 and 57. Slip cast Chetham & Woolley feldspathic dry-bodied stoneware jug with a sprig relief moulding depicting Admiral Lord Nelson holding a speaking trumpet. Unmarked. 1800-1810. Height: 15cm.* (Right) *Plate 57a. Chetham & Woolley feldspathic stoneware jug of c.1806 with a light placed inside it.* PRIVATE COLLECTION

menting the Milan Earthenware to procure a livelihood for himself and Family'.[3] It is not at all clear what 'ornamenting the Milan Earthenwares' means, but it is not inconceivable that Richard was a useful enamel decorator and he may have performed decorating work at the Chetham and Woolley factory prior to leaving it. Interestingly most of the known more elaborately enamelled presentation pieces appear date prior to 1809, the year Richard Woolley left.

There is one other small grouping of Chetham & Woolley jugs, an example of which is illustrated in Plate 55. Jugs of this type are made from the typical 'pearl' feldspathic stoneware body, although subsequent sprig relief decorated items have an underlying principal shape which is slip cast from a plaster mould (Appendix 4) and not turned on a wheel. A resulting feature of

this manufacturing process is that the feldspathic stoneware body is thin and extremely translucent. The jug in Plate 55 is sprig decorated with moulds from the factory specific group illustrated in Plates 38 and 39, and in addition has the common form of handle for Chetham & Woolley jugs shown in Plate 35. These features appearing together validate the inclusion of jugs of this type within the Chetham & Woolley product range.

Jugs of this distinctive shape are of particular interest because they are sometimes decorated with sprig relief scenes which commemorate Admiral Lord Nelson. Another sprig relief decoration often found on these jugs is a ship of the line which is commonly believed to represent HMS *Victory*.[4] If this is the case, it suggests that these pieces were made after October 1805 and are posthumous tributes to Lord Nelson.

6.

'PEARL' STONEWARE MUGS

As was shown with the oak-leaf border group, Chetham & Woolley produced a comprehensive range of useful wares so it is not surprising that they also made mugs from 'pearl' feldspathic stoneware.

Plate 58 shows an example of a mug which matches the Chetham & Woolley 'pearl' feldspathic stoneware of the jugs discussed in the previous chapter. The engine turned decoration at

Plate 58. Feldspathic dry-bodied stoneware mug with a distinctive handle. Sprig decorated with an unusual Chetham & Woolley hunting scene. Engine turned base. Unmarked. 1800-1810. Height: 9.5cm.

PRIVATE COLLECTION

the base is in the same form as the jugs in the first group with sixty-four vertical ridges. More importantly, the mug is sprig relief decorated with an unusual hunting scene which is exactly the same as that found on many of the Chetham & Woolley jugs. The sprig moulds used to make the hunting scene on the mug in Plate 58 are numbers 1, 3, and 6 (see Plates 38 and 39). Plate 59 shows the mug next to a Chetham & Woolley jug; the 'Deep-seated rider' sprig mould scene can be seen on both. There are so many similarities between the mug in Plate 58 and the Chetham & Woolley jugs that it is reasonable to conclude that this mug was also made in the Lane End factory.

Many other examples of these Chetham & Woolley mugs have now been identified. Generally they are decorated around the rim with a blue or brown coloured band, sometimes with the handle line-edged in the same colour. In a few cases colour decoration is entirely absent. An almost universal characteristic feature of Chetham & Woolley mugs of this grouping is the unusual handle design shown in Plate 60. The handle meets the main body at three points giving an appearance which has given rise to the term 'ear with lobe' handle. It is a distinctive, easily recognisable form and seems from the evidence so far available to be factory specific. No mugs have yet been found with this handle which do not also

Plate 59. A Chetham & Woolley feldspathic stoneware jug and mug of the same body. Both are sprig relief decorated with an unusual hunting scene. 1795-1810. Heights: 9.5cm and 20.5cm.   PRIVATE COLLECTION

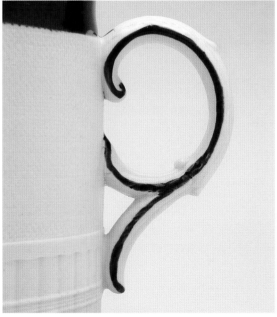

Plate 60. An unusual handle which is typical of Chetham & Woolley feldspathic stoneware mugs.

Plate 61. Chetham & Woolley feldpathic stoneware mug enamelled with a naïve rustic scene in an oval surround. Unmarked. 1800-1810. Height: 9cm. PRIVATE COLLECTION

display other clearly recognisable Chetham & Woolley features, though of course there is always the possibility that a piece with this handle from another factory may yet be found.

Chetham & Woolley mugs were made in several sizes, ranging from 17cm to 6cm. Some were sprig decorated with neo-classical images, others with hunting scenes. Rare examples, such as that shown in Plate 61, have both sprig mould decoration and elaborately painted vignettes similar to the presentation jugs.

Although the 'ear with lobe' handle is almost universally found on Chetham & Woolley mugs there is one example which has been found with a rectangular form of handle as shown in Plate 62. In addition, Chetham & Woolley 'ear with lobe' handle mugs have been discovered which are sprig decorated with hunting scenes composed from the second group of four factory

associated mouldings (Plates 46-49). One such mug is shown in Plates 63-66. It will be shown later that this second group of factory associated hunting sprig moulds were also used in another sector of the Chetham & Woolley feldspathic stoneware range.

There are some rare examples of 'ear with lobe' handle mugs which have more elaborately engine turned bases. Instead of the more common vertical ridges they are decorated with very fine horizontal ribbing interspersed with wider vertical pillars which form a series of horizontally striated oblongs. An engine turning lathe of some sophistication would have been required to achieve this complex decorative finish. Of particular interest is the example in Plate 67. The more elaborate engine turning together with an untypical combination of classical and rustic sprig relief decoration links this mug to a large group of Chetham & Woolley wares which are discussed in Chapter 8.

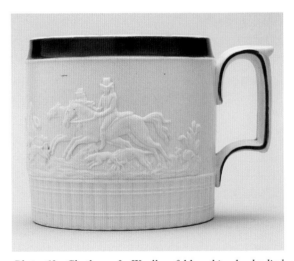

Plate 62. Chetham & Woolley feldspathic dry-bodied stoneware mug sprig decorated with factory associated sprig moulds, but with an untypical rectangular handle. Unmarked. 1800-1810. Height: 7.5cm PRIVATE COLLECTION

Plates 63, 64, 65 and 66. Chetham & Woolley feldspathic stoneware mug sprig decorated with a hunting scene composed of factory associated sprig moulds. Unmarked. 1800-1810. Height: 9cm. PRIVATE COLLECTION

Plate 67. Feldspathic dry-bodied stoneware mug with blue enamel bands and sprig decorated with putti and a rustic boy with a dog. Complex engine turned decoration. Unmarked. 1800-1810. Height: 6cm. WAKEFIELD MUSEUM

7.

PRATT-TYPE WARES

Pratt ware is a somewhat confusing term, but is generally used to describe pieces of creamware and pearlware which are relief moulded and underglazed with enamel, usually in a lively palette of blue, ochre, purple, brown and green.[1]

Although relief decoration is an essential feature of Pratt wares, this has not always been achieved through the use of sprig decoration. The relief effect is more often moulded with the main body and the raised images are the result of slip casting (see Appendix 4).

Plate 68 shows a sub-group assembled from the shards found in the vicinity of the Chetham & Woolley Commerce Street site. Close

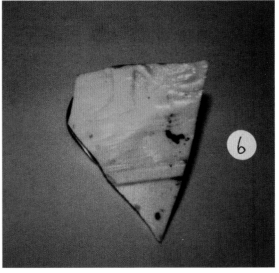

Plate 69. Detail of piece 6 in Plate 68. Slip moulded feldspathic stoneware shard from the group found in the vicinity of the Chetham & Woolley Commerce Street site, Longton.

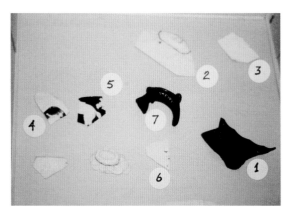

Plate 68. A sub-group of the shards found close to Chetham & Woolley factory.

CITY MUSEUM AND ART GALLERY, STOKE

examination of one of these shards reveals a fragmentary relief moulding of a booted foot and lower leg with a stick-like object protruding behind the boot at calf level. These relief features are not formed by sprig relief decoration, but are integral with the body of the shard, which has been made by slip casting. For many years it

Plate 70. Slip cast feldspathic dry-bodied stoneware jug, thin walled and highly translucent. Sparcely decorated in green, blue and puce enamel. Unmarked. 1800-1815. Height: 10cm.

proved impossible to match this shard with any known complete item, but a feldspathic stoneware jug (Plate 70) has recently been identified which is reminiscent of pieces classified as Pratt ware.

On one side of the jug is a relief moulded country sports theme depicting the netting of partridges, and on the other side a country sportsman is shooting a woodcock. The sportsman wears calf length boots and just ahead of him is his dog, probably a setter, whose hind leg appears behind the sportsman's left boot. The sportsman's boot and the dog's hind leg are a precise match for the combination found on the

Plate 71. Piece of shard placed against matching point on Pratt-type jug. Both are slip cast from feldspathic stoneware. Jug unmarked. 1795-1805. PRIVATE COLLECTION

coincides with that of the majority of the other Chetham & Woolley jugs examined in Chapter 5.

The general form of the type of handle shown in Plate 72 is occasionally seen on both jugs and mugs made by other factories making stoneware at this time. However, there is a particular feature of the general shape which appears to be specifically associated with the Chetham & Woolley factory,

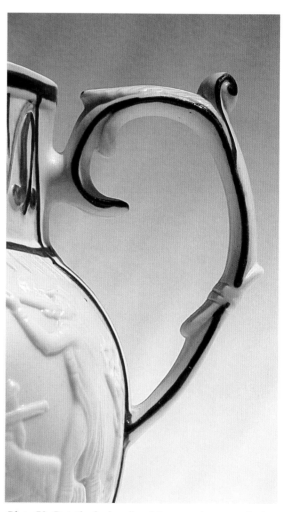

Plate 72. Detail of a handle of the type shown on the jug in Plate 70.

shard (the stick-like object is actually the setter's hind leg). Both the shard and jug are shown in Plate 71.

As discussed in previous chapters, it is likely that these shards are Chetham & Woolley pieces and it is therefore reasonable to conclude that the Pratt type jug could also have been made by this factory. Further weight is given to this conclusion by the fact that the shape of the handle of the jug

Plates 73 and 74. Two feldspathic dry-bodied stoneware Pratt-type jugs, both with a type of handle specifically associated with Chetham & Woolley. Unmarked. 1800-1810. Height: 10cm.   PRIVATE COLLECTION

where it is only used as a handle for jugs. The lower of the two cusps enclosing the stem at the top of the handle projects towards the main body of the jug and is bold in the Chetham & Woolley version. Where this general handle form is found on the jugs or mugs of other makers, the lower cusp is either residual or absent.

Several other Chetham & Woolley feldspathic stoneware Pratt-type jugs have recently been found and two examples are shown in Plates 73 and 74. Although only few jugs of the Chetham & Woolley feldspathic stoneware Pratt-type

range have been discovered, in all cases the enamel decoration is mainly limited to the colour range of blue, green and puce and is relatively subdued in comparison to Pratt ware in general. This is not to say that more ornately coloured pieces will yet be found, however. One reason for hoping that more may be discovered is that it has only recently been established that Chetham & Woolley jugs of this type were made in more than one size. For example, a jug of 19cm in height has just been found which matches the 10cm example shown in Plate 74.

8.
MIST-TYPE WARES

(See also Appendix 5)

(A) OCTAGONAL TEAPOTS AND ASSOCIATED WARES

There are several shards from the group found near the Chetham & Woolley Commerce Street site which can be readily matched to a well known, but previously unattributed category of feldspathic stonewares (Plate 75). The octagonal form and decorative features of these fragments mean that they can easily be identified as coming from a group of elegant octagonal-shaped feldspathic stoneware teapots such as that illustrated in Plate 76.

Plate 76. Octagonal feldspathic stoneware teapot both slip moulded and sprig relief decorated with a hinged cover, 1800-1820. Unmarked. Height 14cm. PRIVATE COLLECTION

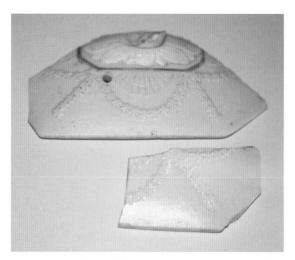

Plate 75. Two shards (Numbers 2 and 3 in Plate 68) from the group found close to the Chetham & Woolley factory.
CITY MUSEUM AND ART GALLERY, STOKE

The main bodies of teapots of this design are partially decorated with raised mouldings created by slip casting. Additional sprig relief decoration has been applied to plain or coloured ground side panels. When compared to the teapot covers in Plates 77 and 78, it is clear to see that the shard

in Plate 75 was also once part of a similar piece. Not only does the octagonal form of the cover coincide, but the raised swag decoration on the smaller shard also matches exactly.

In Plate 79 another feldspathic stoneware shard from the group is shown. This also originates from the same category of octagonal wares. Plate 80 shows how precisely the features remaining on the shard coincide with decorated surfaces of the surviving teapot. Many octogonal teapots of this kind are known and another excellent example is illustrated in Plate 81.[1]

In previous sections other shards found in the same group as those in Plates 75 and 79 have been shown to be derived from other categories of Chetham & Woolley feldspathic stoneware. As all of these shards were discovered in a coherent batch, it is not unreasonable to draw the conclusion that Chetham & Woolley also made the well known group of feldspathic dry-bodied stoneware octagonal teapots.

The teapot in Plate 81 is especially interesting because the base is impressed with the mark 'MIST LONDON' (Plate 82). Normally im-

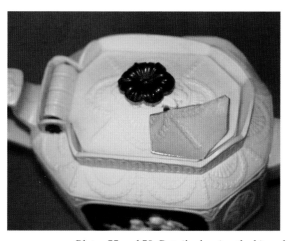

Plates 77 and 78. Details showing the hinged cover of the teapot in Plate 76 and how the shard in Plate 75 matches the pattern and shape of the other cover.

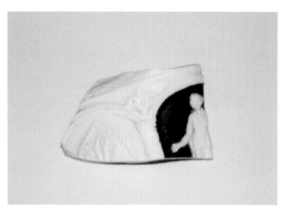

Plate 79. Feldspathic dry-bodied stoneware shard (number 4 in Plate 68) from the group found close to Chetham & Woolley factory.

CITY MUSEUM AND ART GALLERY, STOKE

Plate 81. Octagonal feldspathic stoneware teapot which is both slip moulded and sprig relief decorated. Hinged cover. Marked 'MIST LONDON'. 1800-1820 Height: 14cm. MERSEYSIDE MUSEUM

Plate 80. Detail of the teapot in Plate 76 with the smaller shard in Plate 79.

Plate 82. Detail showing the 'MIST LONDON' mark impressed on the base of the teapot in Plate 81.

pressed marks were used to identify the factory where the item was made, but that is not so in this case. The name comes from James Underhill Mist, but he never had his own factory and was actually a retailer (see Appendix 5).

The MIST mark, impressed in upper case, appears on a considerable number of decorative

feldspathic stoneware pieces. It appears in various different forms: 'MIST', 'J MIST', 'MIST LONDON' and even '82 FLEET STREET LONDON'.[2]

Feldspathic stonewares marked 'MIST' are representative of a much larger group of decorative feldspathic stonewares which are unmarked, but are stylistically identical to the 'MIST' pieces. Unmarked examples range from octagonal teapots and ancillary tea wares, to fine sprig relief decorated jugs, mugs, and bowls, together with ornamental vases of various shapes. The decorative style for all members of this group is completely coherent, and both the marked and unmarked pieces are essentially members of the same group of wares. The uniformity of these marked and unmarked

feldspathic stonewares has given rise to the generic term 'MIST-type', which is applied both to marked and unmarked examples of the wares. It is most probable that only a tiny minority of these pieces, those impressed with the 'MIST' mark, actually passed through James Mist's retail outlet in Fleet Street.

Chetham & Woolley feldspathic stoneware items which are marked 'MIST' may be dated between 1809 and 1815. This is becuase James

Plates 83 and 84. Shell lappet decoration on the teapot in Plate 76 with enlargement.

Plates 85a and 85b. Shell lappet decorative motif transferred to the teapot cover and shoulder when the cover is not hinged.

PRIVATE COLLECTION

Plates 86 and 87. Octogonal feldspathic stoneware covered sucrier and creamer. Unmarked.
1800-1820. Heights: sucrier 13.5cm, creamer 9cm. PRIVATE COLLECTION

Mist could not have marked his name on items until he became the sole proprietor of the retail concern in March 1809, and he was declared bankrupt in April 1815. This time scale largely coincides with the period when Ann Chetham was managing the Chetham & Woolley Commerce Street factory.

Every known example of this type of octagonal teapot, marked or unmarked, has the distinctive decorative feature shown in Plates 83 and 84. This type of decoration has been named the 'shell lappet' border.[3] In the case of the Chetham & Woolley octagonal teapots, this feature was not created by sprig relief decoration, but was achieved by slip casting from an intaglio mould with the feature already in place (see Appendix 4). When the teapot cover is hinged, the shell lappet border always surrounds the bottom of the piece. However, for some teapots within the Chetham & Woolley octagonal group the covers are not hinged, but sit independently within a gallery. In this configuration the shell lappet pattern is transferred onto the cover itself and to the upper shoulder of the teapot, as illustrated in Plates 85a and 85b.

As might be expected, ancillary wares were also made to accompany these attractive octagonal teapots. A covered sucrier and a cream jug which belong within the group are illustrated in Plates 86 and 87 and the distinctive shell lappet border is also found the base of these items.

As mentioned previously, feldspathic stoneware octagonal teapots and ancillary wares within this group are commonly classed as MIST-type wares and the shard evidence argues that they were made at the Chetham & Woolley factory in Commerce Street. All known example of teapots and ancillary wares of this type display the shell lappet border. Conversely, no other feldspathic stoneware is known which has the same shell lappet border. Therefore, the conclusion might persuasively be drawn that the shell lappet border motif is exclusive to the Chetham & Woolley factory. There are also some octagonal teapots of exactly the same shape as the feldspathic stoneware pieces discussed above which are made in basalt stoneware or Egyptian black.[4] The shell lappet decoration is also present on the basalt examples.

Plate 88. Feldspathic shard (marked No.5 in Plate 68) from the group found close to Chetham & Woolley factory.
CITY MUSEUM AND ART GALLERY, STOKE

(B) COLOURED GROUND WARES

Another shard from the group found in the vicinity of the Chetham & Woolley Commerce Street site is shown in Plate 88. It is made of feldspathic stoneware and is sprig relief decorated in white against a brown ground. There is enough of the sprig relief decoration remaining to identify the hind quarters of one of the hunters in 'The Kill', the pattern discussed in Chapter 5. The jug illustrated in Plate 89 has the same brown background as the shard and is sprig relief decorated with 'The Kill' pattern. This also corresponds with the small fragment of pattern on

the surviving shard. It is evident that the jug in Plate 89 is exactly the type of article that the shard in Plate 88 must have come from, which suggests that wares such as this were also made at the Chetham & Woolley factory.

There exists a very large and prolific group of fine feldspathic stoneware pieces – jugs, mugs, spill vases, jardinières, pot-pourri baskets, tobacco jars, ornamental vases and other items – all stylistically alike. The background colour for wares in this group is either brown or blue and, as mentioned previously, some of these pieces are impressed with the 'MIST' mark. 'The Kill' hunting pattern was a common decoration for the MIST-type group, although many other forms of sprig relief decoration were also used. Other than 'The Kill', the majority of the sprig relief designs can be traced back to decorations originally introduced to the dry-bodied stoneware decorative repertoire by either Josiah Wedgwood, to embellish basalt and jasperware, or by John Turner to enhance his special honey coloured stoneware.[5]

There is uniformity in colour for the sprig relief decoration of MIST-type ware. Whereas the ground colour is either brown or blue, the applied sprig relief decoration is always white. In most cases the ground colour covers virtually the whole surface of the piece, but in some instances the sprig decoration is applied within a coloured oval panel and the main body is left as uncoloured stoneware. Some examples of the extensive MIST-type range are given in Plates 90 to 96.

The most commonly used handle found on MIST-type pieces is in the form of a 'C' scroll and spur, though a simpler type also occurs. Both handles are shown on similar jugs in Plate 97 and they also appear on the mugs in Plates 98 and 99.

There are also examples of feldspathic

Plate 89. Brown ground feldspathic stoneware jug sprig relief decorated with 'The Kill'. Unmarked. 1800-1820. Height 14.5cm.   PRIVATE COLLECTION

Plate 90. MIST-type feldspathic stone-ware mug with brown ground, sprig relief decoration of classical figures in raised oval panels. Complex engine turned base. Unmarked. 1800-1820 Height 13cm. PRIVATE COLLECTION

Plate 91. Two typical MIST-type feld-spathic stoneware jugs sprig decorated with 'The Kill'. Complex engine turned base. 1800-1815. Heights 8.5cm and 11cm. PRIVATE COLLECTION

Plate 92. MIST-type feldspathic stoneware trumpet vase sprig decorated with seated classical figures and a classical floral border on a blue ground. Unmarked. 1800-1815. Height 19cm. PRIVATE COLLECTION

Plate 93. MIST-type feldspathic stoneware campana vase with sprig decoration of classical figures within blue ground oval panels and the main body uncloured. Unmarked. 1800-1815. Height 18.5cm. PRIVATE COLLECTION

stoneware jardinières in the MIST style. Originally there would have been a separate accompanying dish stand to prevent water leakage, but these are mostly missing from pieces found today. Two examples of jardinières are given in Plates 100 and 101.

The two principal sprig relief decorative features on the trumpet vases in Plate 102 depict seated figures (male and female), both dressed in classical robes and each playing a lyre. The seated lyre player represents Orpheus, who could tame wild beasts by the magical effect of his wondrous playing, and a small lion can be seen resting quietly beneath his chair. The Orpheus

Plate 94. Group of MIST-type feldspathic stoneware campana vases with sprig decoration of classical figures within blue and brown ground oval panels. Unmarked. 1800-1815. Heights: 18.5cm, 13.5cm and 16.5 cm.

PRIVATE COLLECTION

Plate 95. Two brown ground feldspathic stoneware jugs. The larger one is sprig relief decorated with 'The Kill' and the smaller one has a rustic scene of a boy and dog. The pieces demonstrate the variations in the Chetham & Woolley MIST-type range, both in size and decoration. Unmarked. 1800-1815. Heights: 6.5cm and 24.5cm. PRIVATE COLLECTION

Plate 96. Brown ground MIST-type beaker with classical sprig relief decoration and lower border. 1800-1815 Height 11cm.
BOWES MUSEUM, CASTLE BARNARD.
PHOTOGRAPH: COLIN WYMAN

Plates 98 and 99. Two typical feldspathic stoneware MIST-type mugs sprig decorated with various figures. Complex engine turned base. Different handles are shown. Unmarked 1800-1820. Height 7cm. PRIVATE COLLECTION

Plate 97. Two typical feldspathic stoneware MIST-type jugs sprig decorated with 'The Kill'. Complex engine turned base. Different handle are shown. Unmarked 1800-1820. Heights: 8.5 and 11cm. PRIVATE COLLECTION

Plates 100 and 101. Two MIST-type jardinières sprig relief decorated on a blue ground, one with classical figures (Plate 100) and another with a geometric pattern and classical floral border below the rim (Plate 101). Unmarked. 1800-1820. Height: 10cm. PRIVATE COLLECTION

Plate 102. Two MIST-type feldspathic stoneware trumpet vases with different gounds, both with sprig relief floral borders and figures in classical dress. Unmarked. 1800-1815. Heights: 19cm and 15.5cm PRIVATE COLLECTION

Plate 103. MIST-type feldspathic stoneware vase sprig decorated with classical figures and a classical border around the rim, all on a brown ground. Marked 'J. MIST LONDON'. 1809-1815. Height: 14cm. PRIVATE COLLECTION

Plate 104. Feldspathic stoneware tobacco jar in the MIST style, 1800-1815. Height: 16cm. PRIVATE COLLECTION

sprig mould is often accompanied by a seated female lyre player, representing the Muse Calliope (Orpheus's mother). Uncharacteristically, the representation of Orpheus does not appear in the sprig mould range of either Wedgwood or Turner. Where Orpheus and Calliope do appear on feldspathic stoneware, the two sprig moulds are strongly, though not exclusively, associated with Chetham & Woolley MIST-type wares.

A less common form of ornamental vase is shown in Plate 103. It is impressed marked 'J. MIST LONDON'. MIST-type tobacco jars are

also known and an example of one of these is shown in Plate 104. Spill vases are a rare Chetham & Woolley MIST-type form and examples of these are shown in Plate 105.

The great majority of MIST-type jugs and mugs have fine engine turning around the base. This feature closely resembles the fine engine turning at the base of the small 'ear-with-lobe' mug (Plate 67).

Another typical small MIST-type jug is shown below in Plates 106-108. This jug shares all the main characteristics of the MIST-type group, but the sprig relief decoration is extremely rare. It is

Plate 105. A pair of feldspathic stoneware spill vases in the MIST style. Unmarked. Height: 11cm. 1800-1815.   PRIVATE COLLECTION

a hunting scene which is composed from the second group of four sprigs, as discussed in Chapters 5 and 6 and illustrated in Plates 46-49. The fact that this group of four hunting sprig moulds appear on three different categories of Chetham & Woolley's wares – jugs, mugs, and MIST-type wares – confirms their position within the factory's repertoire.

As can be seen in Plates 92, 100, 101 and 102, many MIST-type pieces are sprig relief decorated with an intricate classical floral border. The same pattern appears on many different types of ware. In Plate 109, for example, it is shown on a jug, a trumpet vase and a jardinière.

Classical borders of this genre were used by many stoneware makers and are particularly well

Plates 106-108. Blue ground MIST-type jug sprig relief decorated with a hunting scene composed of sprig moulds (see Plates 46-49). 1800-1815. Height: 9cm.

PRIVATE COLLECTION

known on the jasperware, basalts and canewares of Wedgwood. Other makers such as Spode and Turner also regularly made use of classical floral borders. However, similar though these floral borders are, differences can be identified between the precise patterns used by different makers. The classical floral border illustrated in Plate 109 is the one most commonly found on Chetham &

Woolley MIST-type wares and it differs from the Wedgwood, Spode and Turner versions. A comparison is shown in Plate 110 between an example of a Chetham & Woolley and a Spode border. The Spode border is at the bottom of the standing spill vase and the inverted jardinière shows the Chetham & Woolley MIST-type border.

Plate 109. Three articles of MIST-type fedspathic stoneware each sprig relief decorated with the same classical floral border. Unmarked. 1800-1820
PRIVATE COLLECTION

Plate 110. Different classical floral borders used by makers of decorative feldspathic stoneware. On the right a Spode spill vase and on the left an inverted Chetham & Woolley MIST-type jardinière. 1800-1815.
PRIVATE COLLECTION

Plate 111. Gloss-black stoneware teapot with bird-neck spout and floral surround. Impressed 'CHETHAM'. 1820-1830. Height: 9.5cm.   PRIVATE COLLECTION

Although this classical border is frequently found on Chetham & Woolley MIST-type feldspathic stonewares, it cannot be claimed as entirely exclusive to their factory. Plate 111 shows a gloss-black stoneware teapot dating from about 1830 which is marked 'CHETHAM'. Gloss-black ware of this type was made from the 1820s onwards by several manufacturers. A similar teapot is shown in Plate 113, but this one bears the mark of 'CYPLES', another Lane End manufacturer. Plate

Plate 112. Detail showing 'CHETHAM' mark on the base of Plate 111.

Plate 113. Gloss-black stoneware teapot with classical floral border. Impressed 'CYPLES'. 1820-1830. Height: 10cm.   PRIVATE COLLECTION

114 shows that the classical floral border around the central body of the 'CYPLES' teapot is precisely the same as the border on the MIST-type wares discussed above and illustrated in Plates 109 and 110.

It is possible that this particular form of classical border was exclusive to the Chetham & Woolley factory in earlier periods, but clearly this was not the case from c.1820 onwards. It

therefore cannot be assumed that other manufacturers did not also use this border on their own feldspathic stoneware at earlier times, though no such examples have yet been found. Notwithstanding the latter consideration, this classical floral border is in nearly all cases a reliable aid to identifying MIST-type feldspathic stonewares made by the Chetham & Woolley factory.

Plate 114. Details of classical floral design on the teapot in Plate 113.

The shell lappet border decoration has already been examined closely (Plates 83 and 84) as a moulded decorative motif on the Chetham & Woolley octagonal teapots and also on ancillary wares (Plates 76, 81, 85, 86 and 87). In the case of the Chetham & Woolley octagonal wares the raised shell lappet border was an integral part of the slip moulded body and was not the result of sprig relief decoration. However, the same design does also appear as sprig relief decoration on other examples of Chetham & Woolley MIST-type feldspathic stonewares. For example, the blue ground MIST-type beaker in Plate 115 has a sprig relief decorated shell lappet border around its rim. This feature coincides precisely with that found on the octagonal teapots discussed previously, but, to reiterate, in this case it is sprig relief moulded, whereas the same decorative motif on the octagonal teapot is achieved by slip casting.

Another extremely rare feldspathic stoneware MIST-type article is the cup and saucer illustrated in Plate 116. Again the shell lappet border sprig

Plate 115. Feldspathic stoneware MIST-type beaker sprig relief decorated with the seated figures of Orpheus and Calliope. Unmarked. 1800-1815. Height: 9cm.

Plate 116. Feldspathic stoneware MIST-type teacup and saucer of bute shape with sprig relief decoration of domestic and classical figures on brown ground roundels with shell lappet borders also against a brown ground. Unmarked. 1810-1815. Height: 14cm.

PRIVATE COLLECTION

Plate 117. Shell lapett decoration sprig relief decoration on the inverted teacup (Plate 116) next to the slip moulded form at the base of an octaganol feldspathic teapot (see also Plate 76).

relief decoration appears around the rim of the cup and the outer upward flange of the saucer.

The correspondence between the shell lappet sprig relief decoration on the cup in Plate 116 with the slip moulded decoration on and the octagonal feldspathic teapot (also Plate 76) is demonstrated by the juxtaposition of the two in Plate 117. The shell lappet border is also shown on the Chetham & Woolley MIST-type campana vase in Plate 118.

The shell lappet motif appears on the campana vase in Plate 118 as a sprig relief decorative band around the upper face of the base. Since the slip

moulded shell lapett border has been shown to be specifically associated with Chetham & Woolley feldspathic stoneware MIST-type octagonal teapots, it is entirely consistent to associate the sprig relief form of this decoration with the same factory. The presence of the sprig relief moulded shell lapett border therefore provides further verification that the MIST-type campana vases such as these were produced by the Chetham & Woolley factory. A representative group of similar feldspathic stoneware campana vases is shown in Plate 119.

Several campana vases and other Chetham &

Plate 118. Feldspathic stoneware MIST-type campana vase with sprig relief decoration in brown ground roundels with shell lappet border around the foot (also against a brown ground). Unmarked. 1810-1815. Height: 15cm. PRIVATE COLLECTION

Plate 119. A representative group of Chetham & Woolley MIST-type feldspathic stoneware campana vases. Unmarked. 1800-1810. PRIVATE COLLECTION

Woolley feldspathic stoneware MIST-type pieces are sprig relief decorated with an interesting image refering to Admiral Lord Nelson. A typical example of the sprig mould in question, but from a MIST-type teapot is shown in Plate 120.

Britannia stands holding a trident and facing her is the winged figure of Fame writing the names 'Howe' and 'Nelson' on an oval tablet. The juxtaposition of these two names might at first sight be somewhat puzzling. Admiral Lord Howe had won a famous naval victory against a superior French fleet in June 1794, which became known as 'The Glorious First of June'. Howe was also responsible for suppressing the Spithead Mutiny of 1797. His career culminated in his becoming Admiral of the Fleet. He died in 1799.

The linking of Howe's name with Nelson's on a commemorative sprig moulding would not be easy to explain after his death, unless it was to acknowledge his important victory of June 1794. However, by the time Nelson himself had become famous, Howe was not the only British admiral other than Nelson who had succeeded in battle. Famous naval victories had been won by other accomplished admirals, such as Jervis at Cape St. Vincent and Duncan at Camperdown (both 1797) and these intervened between 'The Glorious First of June' and Nelson's rise to prominence. The presence of Howe's name with Nelson's can be better understood in respect to Howe's superior rank in the naval hierarchy.

These considerations strongly suggest that the sprig relief decoration appearing on certain Chetham & Woolley MIST-type feldspathic stonewares was most likely to have originally been commissioned to commemorate Nelson's outstanding victory at the Battle of the Nile on 1 August, 1798. The appearance of an Egyptian style obelisk between the standing figures of Britannia and Fame supports this proposition.

Plate 120. Representative example of a sprig relief moulding which appears on several Chetham & Woolley MIST-type feldspathic stonewares illustrating Fame writing the names 'Howe' and 'Nelson' on the tablet of fame before a standing figure of Britannia. 1800-1810.

PRIVATE COLLECTION

Since Howe was Admiral of the Fleet in 1798, the linking of his name with Nelson's would have been entirely appropriate in recognition that he was Nelson's ultimate commander. Also it is noteworthy that Howe's name appears above Nelson's on Fame's tablet, again reflecting a positioning appropriate for a superior officer. In later years Nelson's claim to the higher positioning on the tablet of fame would have exceeded Howe's and the joining of Howe's name with Nelson's at any time after Howe's death in 1799 would be difficult to justify.

As was discussed previously, the 'MIST' mark is found on only a minority of wares in the MIST-type category and the marked items are likely only to have been made within the six

Plate 121. Sprig relief decoration on a Chetham & Woolley feldspathic stoneware MIST-type campana vase in the form of a medallion against a brown ground with a banner above bearing the word 'TRAFALGAR'. 1806-1815. Height: 19cm. PRIVATE COLLECTION

years between 1809 to 1815. But the implication of the Howe and Nelson sprig relief decoration in Plate 120 is that unmarked MIST-type wares must have been made by the original Chetham & Woolley partnership a decade before 1809. This conclusion is supported by the presence of commemorative sprig relief decoration on other MIST-type pieces which celebrates Nelson's final victory and demise at Trafalgar in 1805, as shown in Plate 121.

It is implausible that sprig relief decoration referring to Trafalgar would have first appeared in 1809, when Chetham & Woolley Mist-type items would first have been marked 'MIST' (see

Appendix 5). It is more likely that they were made without the 'MIST' mark during the original partnership of James Chetham and Richard Woolley. After James's death in 1807 the partnership continued with his widow, Ann, taking his place and the factory probably supplied a number of retail outlets, including Abbott & Mist (see Appendix 5). As mentioned previously, most pieces actually marked 'MIST' would have been made by Ann Chetham, after November 1809, when she was in sole charge of the factory following Richard Woolley's departure. Whilst making marked pieces for James Mist, Ann Chetham probably also supplied other retailers

Plates 122 and 123. Chetham & Woolley MIST-type feldspathic stoneware sprig decorated jug with portraits of Wellington and Blucher in white rimmed surrounds against a blue ground. Unmarked. c.1815. Height: 15cm. PRIVATE COLLECTION

with unmarked MIST-type feldspathic stone-wares, and she is likely to have continued that trade even after James Mist's bankruptcy in April 1815. Therefore, the conclusion is that MIST-type wares were a long standing element within the Chetham & Woolley product range and that the marked pieces which give the group its name formed only a minority of MIST-type products. The pieces actually marked 'MIST' were almost certainly made for only six years between 1809 and 1815, whereas the unmarked MIST-type stonewares were made during a much longer period of time.

There is no doubt that Chetham & Woolley MIST-type production continued after the collapse of James Mist's retail enterprise. The jug illustrated in Plates 122 and 123 is another commemorative piece with the MIST-type group. This jug is sprig relief decorated with a portrait on one side of the Duke of Wellington and on the other of Blucher, the commander of the Prussian forces at the Battle of Waterloo. The piece was obviously made to commemorate Waterloo and can thus be dated no earlier than June 1815. Though rare, the combination of these portraits is known on other MIST-type pieces, on mugs as well as jugs.[6] Since it is known that James Mist was in financial difficulties by June 1815, prior to his bankruptcy in November 1815, it is very unlikely though not impossible that he was involved in the sale of commemorative MIST-type pieces like these.[7] The jug illustrated in Plates 124-126 was certainly made outside the time range of James Mist's business activity.

Although it lacks the usual coloured ground, this jug can be unmistakably grouped with the Chetham & Woolley MIST–type wares on account of various other features. Again it is a

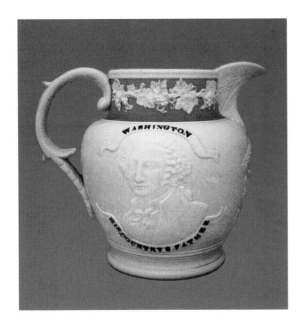

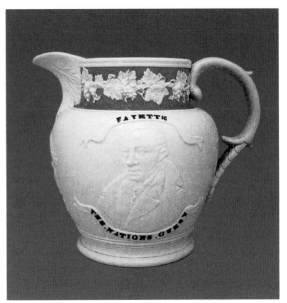

Plates 124-126. Chetham & Woolley MIST-type feldspathic stoneware jug sprig decorated with portraits of Washington and La Fayette with the captions beneath reading 'His County's Father' and 'The Nation's Guest' respectively. Unmarked. c.1824. Height: 16.5cm.

LOCATION UNKNOWN

*Plate 127. Pair of feldspathic stoneware MIST-type jugs sprig relief decorated with 'The Kill'
against a blue ground. Unmarked. 1810-1815. Heights: 9cm and 13cm.* PRIVATE COLLECTION

commemorative piece. One side has the sprig decorated portrait of George Washington with the caption beneath reading 'His Country's Father'. Under the lip is the American bald eagle and shield with thirteen stars arching above, representing the original United States, and on the other side a is portrait of Lafayette with the caption beneath reading 'The Nation's Guest'.

The piece must have been made specifically for the nineteenth century American market when the factory was under the control of Jonathan Lowe Chetham, the son of James and Ann, and his partner at the time, John Robinson. Lafayette had assisted the American colonies in their struggle with the British during the War of Independence. After Britain's defeat he returned to France, but he later re-visited America as an honoured guest of state in August 1824. There can be no doubt that this Chetham factory jug was produced to commemorate that event. It is

not clear that MIST-type wares continued to be made by the factory into the later 1820s and so this jug may mark the final period of production for wares of the MIST-type.

A fascinating note in relation to the factory's MIST-type wares has come to light through the discovery of some old family photographs by Mrs Elaine Chetham (a direct descendant of the firm's founding partner, James Chetham). Plate 127 below shows a typical pair of Chetham & Woolley MIST-type blue ground jugs both sprig relief decorated with 'The Kill' pattern. An identical pair of feldspathic stoneware MIST-type jugs sprig decorated with the same pattern against a blue ground can also be seen sitting on the right hand end of a mantelpiece shelf shown in Plates 128 and 129.

This match between two pairs of MIST-type jugs would be of little interest were it not for the fact that the mantelpiece once belonged to Helen

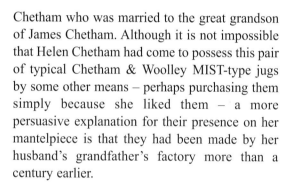

Plates 128 and 129. Mantle shelf with two blue ground Chetham & Woolley MIST-type feldspathic stoneware jugs.

Chetham who was married to the great grandson of James Chetham. Although it is not impossible that Helen Chetham had come to possess this pair of typical Chetham & Woolley MIST-type jugs by some other means – perhaps purchasing them simply because she liked them – a more persuasive explanation for their presence on her mantelpiece is that they had been made by her husband's grandfather's factory more than a century earlier.

(C) OVAL CARTOUCHE GROUP

In the first part of this chapter it was shown that a well known group of finely made octagonal feldspathic stoneware teapots formed part of the MIST-type product range of the Chetham & Woolley factory. A close stylistic affinity exists between these octagonal teapots and a large group of other finely fashioned feldspathic stonewares, a group predominantly consisting of jugs in various sizes. One of these jugs is shown below in Plate 130 side by side with the Chetham & Woolley MIST-type octagonal teapot illustrated in Plate 76.

The similarity of the decoration between the two pieces in Plate 130 is obvious. The contrast of white sprig mouldings on brown ground panels set within a honey coloured feldspathic body is a common characteristic of both. A substantial grouping of jugs is known of the type shown in Plate 130 and all of them have sprig decorated brown ground oval panels. Two typical jugs of this group are illustrated in Plates 131 and 132. Some jugs within the group are covered and in these cases a strainer is normally found behind the beak.

The uniformity of decorative treatment within a group of oval cartouche jugs is demonstrated in Plate 134 and supports the notion of a separate classification for wares of this type: the 'oval cartouche group'. A rare example of the jug in Plate 135, dated 1810, implies that this piece was made when the factory was under the sole control of Ann Chetham following the dissolution in 1809 of her partnership with Richard Woolley.

The ground colour for the panels within oval cartouche group was not always brown. There are rare examples of ovals with a light blue ground as in the case of the fine bowl in Plate 136 and the tobacco jar in Plate 137. However although there

Plate 130. Finely made feldspathic stoneware jug sprig relief decorated with classical figures in brown ground oval cartouches next to the Chetham & Woolley MIST-type octagonal teapot also illustrated in Plate 76. Unmarked. 1800-1815. Heights: teapot 14cm, jug 20cm.

PRIVATE COLLECTION

Plates 131 and 132. Two finely made feldspathic stoneware jugs sprig relief decorated with classical figures in brown ground oval cartouches similar to the jug illustrated in Plate 130. Unmarked. 1800-1815. Plate 131: Height: 12cm; Plate 132: Height: 16cm.   PRIVATE COLLECTION

Plate 133. A finely made covered feldspathic stoneware jug sprig relief decorated with classical figures in brown ground oval cartouches. Strainer behind the beak. Unmarked. 1800-1815. Height: 17.5cm.
PRIVATE COLLECTION

Plate 134. Group of oval cartouche feldspathic stoneware jugs. All unmarked. 1800-1815. Heights ranging from 8cm to 20cm.   PRIVATE COLLECTION

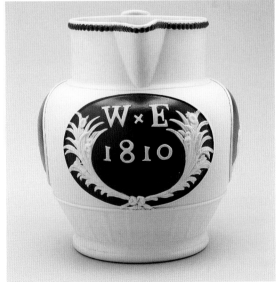

Plate 135. A finely made feldspathic stoneware jug sprig relief decorated with classical figures in brown ground oval cartouches and with the date 1810 beneath the initials 'W x E'. Unmarked. 1810. Height: 16cm.

PRIVATE COLLECTION

Plate 136. *Finely made feldspathic stoneware bowl sprig relief decorated with classical figures in blue ground oval cartouches. Unmarked. 1800-1815. Height: 9cm.*
PRIVATE COLLECTION

are these rare blue ground exceptions, by far the majority of the known pieces in the oval cartouche group have a brown ground.

One very unusual example of the group is a large bowl marked 'MIST' with the Fleet Street address. This means that it was made between 1809 and 1815 as discussed in Section 3.(5)(b) above. Another rare example of an oval cartouche group jardinière, shown in Plate 140, is of particular interest. In addition to the sprig relief

Plate 137. *A covered feldspathic stoneware tobacco pot sprig relief decorated with classical figures and commemorative compositions in blue ground oval cartouches. Initialled and dated 1810. Unmarked. Height: 15cm.*
PRIVATE COLLECTION

Plates 138 and 139. Large feldspathic stoneware oval cartouche group bowl with classical figures against a brown ground. Marked 'J MIST 82 FLEET STREET LONDON'. 1809-1815. Height: 11cm. CITY MUSEUM AND ART GALLERY, STOKE

decoration within brown ground oval cartouches, the jardinniere is sprig decorated with the same factory associated shell lappet border as is found slip moulded on the MIST-type feldspathic stoneware octagonal teapots, discussed above in 3.5(a) and illustrated in Plate 117. The border also appears on the MIST-type beaker in Plate 115, the cup and saucer in Plate 116, and the campana vase in Plate 118. As has been explored earlier, the shell lappet border provides a useful identifying link between these various elements of the Chetham & Woolley factory's output.

Plate 140. Oval cartouche group feldspathic stoneware jardinière shown on the left inverted next the teapot shown in Plate 76, both with shell lappet borders. Unmarked. 1810-1815. Heights: teapot 14cm, jardinière 13cm. PRIVATE COLLECTION

9.

MISCELLANEOUS

CANDLESTICKS AND VINE DECORATION

Candlesticks were also part of the Chetham & Woolley fedspathic stoneware product range. Two examples are known which are impress marked 'CHETHAM & WOOLLEY'.

Other examples of unmarked feldspathic stoneware candlesticks are known, all corresponding very closely in shape and texture with the marked examples in Plate 142. One pair is illustrated in Plate 143 and two pairs in Plate 144. The two pairs of candlesticks shown in Plate 144 each have dark puce monochrome enamel decoration around the base composed of vine leaves and bunches of grapes. Vine leaf and grape decoration was a popular decorative motif for many ceramic wares in the period. It was used by several manufacturers on a variety of materials, particularly creamware.

The feldspathic stoneware jugs shown in Plate 145 is also decorated with a vine and grape border around the neck, in this case in polychrome. This jug is sprig relief decorated with a hunting scene composed from the sprig moulds associated with the Chetham & Woolley factory as discussed in 3(2) and illustrated in Plates 38 and 39.

A closely matching comparison can be made between the vine leaf and grape decoration around the neck of the presentation jug in Plate

Plates 141. A single feldspathic stoneware candlestick, enamel decorated and marked 'CHETHAM & WOOLLEY'. Height: 12.5cm. NEWARK MUSEUM, NEW JERSEY

Plate 142. Pair of feldspathic stoneware candlesticks, enamel decorated and marked 'CHETHAM & WOOLLEY'. c1800. Height: 11cm. PRIVATE COLLECTION

is attached to the vine by its stalk and then the vine itself passes behind the middle of the next leaf in the series. This sequence of positioning for the vine leaves is exactly the same in the case of the polychrome decoration around the neck of the jug in Plate 145. The uniformity of the vine leaves is shown in Plates 146 and 147.

The decorative links by which the grapes are

Plates 143 and 144. Feldspathic stoneware candlesticks, all enamel decorated. Unmarked. c1800. Heights: 11cm. PRIVATE COLLECTION

145 and the monochrome vine leaf and grape decoration around the feet of the candlesticks in Plate 144. The sequence and positioning of the vine leaves and the way in which the grapes are attached to the vine are the same for the decoration on all of these items.

In the case of the monochrome decoration on all of the candlesticks in Plate 144 one vine leaf

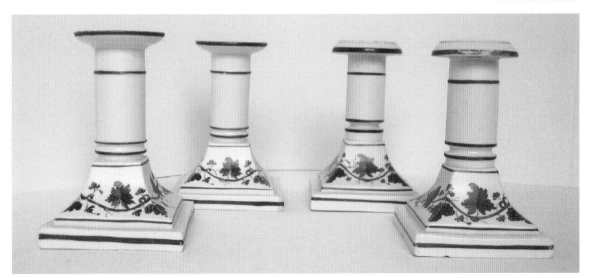

Plate 145. Chetham & Wolley feldspathic stoneware presentation jug sprig decorated with a hunting scene composed of sprig moulds (see Plate 39). Unmarked. 1795-1810. Height: 20.5cm.   PRIVATE COLLECTION

attached to the vine between the leaves are also the same for both the candlesticks and the jug. This is illustrated in Plates 148 and 149, where it can be seen that both for the candlestick monochrome decoration and the jug polychrome decoration a

Plate 146. Base of one of the candlesticks in Plate 144 with monochrome vine leaf and grape bunch enamel decoration.

double loop connects one bunch of grapes to the vine whilst an 'S' stroke connects the next bunch.

The decorative detail of both the positioning of the vine leaves onto the vine and for the links by which grapes are attached is the same on both the jug in Plate 145 and the candlesticks in Plate 144. This exact correlation of between different categories of ware cannot have been accidental. This suggests that for both the presentation jug and the two pairs of candlesticks, the decoration was applied in the same establishment and, if not by the same hand, was executed under the same supervision.

The vine and grape enamel decoration with exactly these features is found on other Chetham & Woolley feldspathic stoneware pieces, for example around the neck of the covered jug in Plate 52. Since it appears to have been applied to different groups of items in precisely the same format, it offers a helpful associating feature for wares from the factory.

As discussed in section 3 (2) in the regard to the more elaborate enamel decoration of Chetham & Woolley presentation jugs, it is not known whether the vine and grape enamel decoration was executed in-house or by outside workers. However, since the detailed arrangement of this border is consistent between different categories of Chetham & Woolley wares and differs from similar formats of vine and grape decoration used by other makers, it it is likely that it was done in-house. It is implausible that an outside decorating establishment would have maintained this specific border type as a service exclusively for the Chetham & Woolley factory. Also, if an outside decorator was buying plain wares to decorate for his own trade then it is likely that he would also have decorated items from other factories with the same design. To date no wares in this same format have been found, other than those which can be attributed to Chetham & Woolley.

Plate 147. Neck of jug in Plate 145 with polychrome vine leaf and grape bunch enamel decoration.

Plates 148 and 149. Neck of jug in Plate 145 with a candlestick from the group in Plate 144 placed on top to show that the decorative links joining the bunches of grapes to the vine are the same.

Plates 150 and 151. Set of three feldspathic stoneware obelisks with enamel decorated columns on blue edged square socles. On the face of each of these is a roundel; three of them are sprig decorated with classical figures and the fourth is enamel painted with a simple rustic scene. Unmarked. Heights: 25.5cm and 28cm. 1800-1810. YORK MUSEUM

OBELISKS AND CHERUBS

In recent years attention has been paid to a small group of feldspathic stoneware obelisks. These are extremely rare objects and most of the known examples are shown in Plates 150 to 154.

The complete set of three obelisks (Plates 150 and 151) are skilfully decorated in an extensive enamel palette with violins and trumpets on some faces and various military accoutrements on others. Those in Plates 153 and 154 are skilfully decorated with floral spays.

However, it is the plinths or socles upon which the obelisks themselves stand which are of particular interest. Each of the four faces is decorated with a raised oval cartouche. Three of the raised oval cartouches are sprig relief decorated with classical figures and the fourth is painted with a primitive rustic scene in lively enamels.

Plate 152. Two feldspathic stoneware obelisks, the columns of which are decorated in marbled enamels and stand on blue edged square socles. On the face of each socle is a roundel sprig decorated with classical figures on a dark blue ground. Unmarked. Heights: 25.5cm and 28cm. 1800-1810. PRIVATE COLLECTION

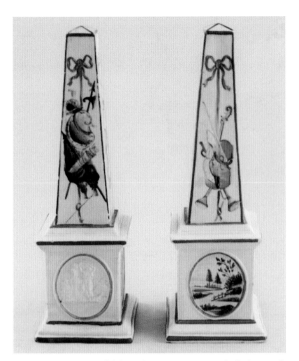

Plate 153. Two feldspathic stoneware obelisks with enamel decorated columns on blue edged square socles. On each face is a roundel; three are sprig decorated with classical figures and the fourth is enamel painted with a simple rustic scene. Unmarked. Height: 25.5cm. 1800-1810. Location unknown

The pair of socles shown in Plate 154 are clearly of the same type. Indeed the plinths of all the shorter obelisks correspond in size, shape and decoration, and they provide a useful clue for identifying the maker of two other exceptional feldspathic stoneware pieces.

Two almost identical and most interesting feldpathic stoneware items are illustrated in Plates 155 and 156. Each is composed of the upper torso and head of a winged cherub mounted on a square socle.[1]

The feldspathic stoneware winged cherub heads bear a close affinity with earlier

realisations of the theme one example of which is shown in Plate 157. This is a porcelain head, probably part of a larger figure, and was made at the Chelsea factory in about 1745.

The feldspathic stoneware heads in Plates 155, 156 and the Chelsea porcelain example in Plate 157 are most probably based on an earlier seventeenth century model after François Duquesnoy, 'Il Fiammingo'. Their original provenance may well be have been earlier still.[2]

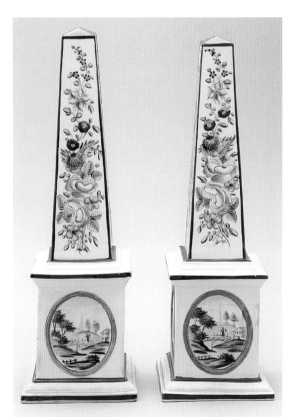

Plate 154. Two feldspathic stoneware obelisks with enamel decorated columns on blue edged square socles. On each face is a roundel; three are sprig decorated with classical figures and the fourth is enamel painted with a simple rustic scene. Impress marked 'CHETHAM & Co.', 1800-1810. Height: 25.5cm.

Plates 155 and 156. Two identical feldspathic stoneware figures, each composed of the torsos of winged cherubs mounted on blue edged square socles. On the face of each is an oval roundel, three of which are sprig decorated with classical figures; the fourth is enamel painted with a simple rustic scene. Unmarked. Height: 25.5cm. 1800-1810.

PLATE 155: PRIVATE COLLECTION. PLATE 156: VICTORIA AND ALBERT MUSEUM

Examples of similar heads are known in plaster and other materials such the brilliantly carved ivory shown in Plate 158. The correspondence between the Chelsea porcelain head in Plate 157 and the feldspathic stoneware examples in Plates 155 and 156 is demonstrated below in Plates 159 and 160.

It is obvious from even a casual observation that the socles upon which the feldspathic stoneware winged cherub heads stand in Plates 155 and 156 closely resemble those supporting the obelisks examined above in Plates 150 -154. Closer examination and precise measurement reveals that the socles are from identical moulds. By merging two images of the socles, one from a winged cherub and one from an obelisk, eventually a single image is formed. This is demonstrated in Plates 161 to 164. Plate 161 shows a winged cherub and an obelisk side by side, Plate 162 shows their socles. The winged cherub and the obelisk were carefully photographed separately with images exactly the

Plate 157. Porcelain head of cherub, possibly part of a larger figure, made by the Chelsea factory c.1745. Height: 5cm.   VICTORIA AND ALBERT MUSEUM

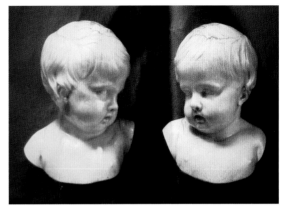

Plate 158. Carved ivory head of cherub. Date, dimemsions and location unknown.

same size. The images were then slowly merged together (Plate 163), and are finally shown to overlap perfectly in Plate 164.

Given this exact correspondence it is reasonable to conclude that whichever factory made the feldspathic stoneware obelisks also made the mounted winged cherubs. The base of the socle from the obelisk in Plate 161 is shown below in Plate 165 and the mark 'CHETHAM & Co.' is clearly impressed.

The conclusion may therefore be drawn that the feldspathic stoneware cherubs heads and obelisks shown here were all made at the Chetham & Woolley Commerce Street factory in Lane End.

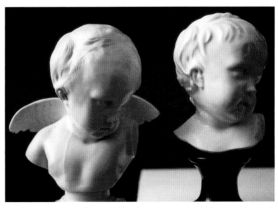

Plates 159 and 160. Feldspathic porcelain winged cherub head and torso in Plate 156 placed beside the Chelsea porcelain head in Plate 157.

Plate 161. Winged cherub in Plate 156 beside one of the obelisks in Plate 154.

Plate 162. Detail of the socles in Plate 161.

Plate 163. Same size images of the socles in Plate 162 are slowly merged.

(Above right) Plate 164. The separate images in Plate 163 merge into one.

Plate 165. Base of obelisk socle in Plate 161 impressed with the 'CHETHAM & Co'. mark

Plate 166. Feldspathic stoneware bust of Admiral Lord Duncan. Impress marked 'CHETHAM AND WOOLLEY, LANE END'. Dated 1798. Height: 60cm.

VICTORIA AND ALBERT MUSEUM

ADMIRAL DUNCAN BUSTS

The attribution of so numerous and varied a range of wares to the Chetham & Woolley enterprise as has been presented in the previous sections implies that the factory was of the first importance. There can be little doubt that Chetham & Woolley would have been numbered amongst the most highly regarded potters of their time, at least in relation to the manufacturing of items from feldspathic stoneware. Even if there was no other evidence were available, there are two surviving examples of craftsmanship which would alone validate this seemingly extravagant claim for the importance of the Chetham & Woolley factory.

Illustrated in Plate 166 is a life size bust of

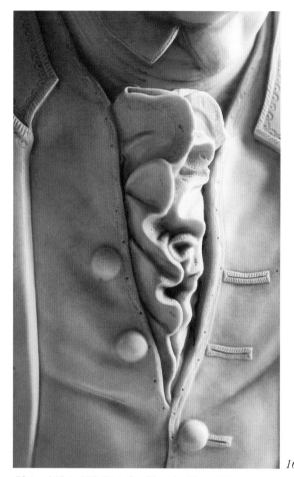

167

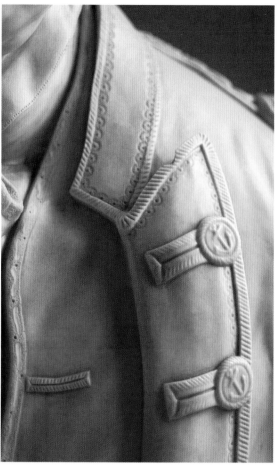

168

Plates 167 to 170. Details of bust in Plate 166.

Admiral Lord Viscount Duncan. It is one of two known examples[3] and stands on its own pedestal. The whole figure is modelled in beautifully toned ivory pearl feldspathic stoneware.

The bust in Plates 166 and 167 is housed in the Vicoria and Albert Musem and once belonged to the great Victorian ceramic historian, William Chaffers. He described it as 'A beautifully modelled bust and pedestal of this fine material.' On the pedestal the following dedication is inscribed:

ADMIRAL LORD VISCOUNT DUNCAN, WHO DEFEATED THE DUTCH FLEET, COMMANDED, BY ADMIRAL DE WINTER OFF THE COAST OF HOLLAND ON WEDNESDAY, 11th OCTOBER 1797[4]

The quality of the modelling is of the highest order and Plates 168-171 demonstrate the excellent workmanship of the tunic, ruff, epaulette and

169

170

pigtail. Inside the pedestal is the date 1798. Only a manufacturer of the highest competence and commercial ability could have produced such an outstanding tribute so soon after the event. This is a brilliant standard of craftsmanship and is maintained throughout the piece. Even without all the other evidence presented in the preceding sections, this bust of Admiral Duncan alone might be considered sufficient to place Chetham & Woolley amongst the foremost ceramic manufacturers of their period.

Plate 171. Impressed mark of 'CHETHAM AND WOOLLEY, LANE END' on the pedestal of the bust in Plate 166.

CONCLUSION

The intention of this work has been to show that the factory of Chetham & Woolley at Commerce Street, Lane End in Staffordshire deserves to be ranked alongside the finest potters of those in existence at the end of the eighteenth and the beginning of the nineteenth centuries. In addition to working with more traditional products, 'Earthenware in general and Egyptian Black', the brothers-in-law James Chetham and Richard Woolley probably invented and certainly introduced an important new ceramic material to the potteries of Staffordshire, the 'pearl' feldspathic stoneware. From this they produced items such as teapots, coffee pots, small tea ware jugs, sucriers, larger hunting-scene jugs, presentation jugs, a wide assortment of mugs, candlesticks, decorative obelisks, and an enormously extensive range of both useful and decorative wares which have been termed by some auction houses as 'MIST-type'.

James Chetham and Richard Woolley established their partnership in the early 1790s just at the time when an increasingly receptive 'middling class' market for decorative artefacts, including ceramics, was developing. The attractive new 'pearl' feldspathic stoneware material was an excellent product with which they could exploit these growing opportunities. Their business 'start-up' was clearly a great success and continued so after James's death in 1807 under the guidance of his wife, Anne, and

later with the involvement of their son, Jonathan Lowe. The extent and complexity of the diverse range of feldspathic stonewares which the factory developed is illustrated throughout this book. Such a range could only have been produced by a factory in the first rank of the ceramic industry.

However, the introduction to the market of 'pearl' feldspathic stoneware would not in itself have been sufficient to achieve such success; the factory also flourished because of its consistently excellent design. Fine styling is displayed in both the attractive character of Chetham & Woolley's more utilitarian wares, such as hunting-pattern jugs, and in the sophisticated forms of their more decorative items, as shown in the MIST-type range. The elegance of these latter decorative wares and the technical excellence of the sprig decoration are quite outstanding, and are matched by few other factories. But it was not only in serving more general markets that Chetham & Woolley succeeded. As was referred to earlier, the cherub figures in Plates 155 and 156 owe their origin to a much earlier design of long and distinguished lineage. There must have been some resource within the Chetham & Woolley business which was conscious of such refinements and provided the stimulus for this tasteful work. It suggests an exceptionally sensitive eye combined with high technical competence.

Even more astonishing are the life-size busts

of Admiral Lord Duncan. The famous Victorian writer on ceramics, William Chaffers, described an example which he owned as 'A beautifully-modelled bust and pedestal of this fine material'. These busts are of superb quality and display extraordinarily sensitive and accomplished modelling, as shown in Plates 167-170. They are dated 1798, only a few years after the Chetham & Woolley factory was established, and yet they must stand as one of the great achievements of the ceramic industry of that time.

Though it is difficult to understand how a ceramic factory with such outstanding achievements could have been so little remembered, it nonetheless seems to be the case with regard to Chetham & Woolley. Perhaps industrial activity counts for little in the cultural consciousness of our society. When a firm ceases to work, memory of it generally quickly evaporates. Where little documentary evidence survives, or, in the case of ceramics, where very few pieces are marked with the maker's name, this process perhaps becomes more rapid. It is a salient point in the case of the Chetham & Woolley enterprise that even direct descendants

of the co-founder, James Chetham, who are alive today, did not know that their forbears had once been potters. This discovery was made only as a result of a family genealogical study begun by one of the descendants.

However, even if they are forgotten, potters leave durable traces of their work. There must be many more surviving Chetham & Woolley pieces waiting to be discovered in the stockrooms of dealers, in private collections or in obscure museum cupboards (the source of several items described here).

The factory's products are worthy of serious attention. A majority of the pieces examined in this book were made during the period of the Napoleonic Wars when Britain was fighting for survival against her most formidable Continental foe. This perhaps somewhat impaired the customary influence of Continental taste upon British decorative artefacts. As a result the feldspathic stonewares made by Chetham & Woolley from 1793 to 1825 may be seen as reflecting a solid yet sound English style. They were regarded, as Simeon Shaw reminds us 'in general estimation of all ranks of society'.[1]

POSTSCRIPT

During a visit with the English Ceramic Circle to the United States in May 2010, three additional interesting feldspathic stoneware items were found, two certainly attributable to Chetham & Woolley and the third perhaps so.

The first item, from a private collection, is a larger helmet-shaped cream jug within the Oak Leaf Border group illustrated in Plate 173. The finely lined blue edging is enhanced by the careful painting in green and blue of the large and small leaf decoration, which is relief moulded, on the shoulder of this so far unique example. The other two discoveries were both made at Historic Deerfield in Massachusetts. One is part of the foundation's collection and the other belongs to a private individual living in the town.

Plate 172 shows a rare and late Chetham & Woolley MIST-type jug. It is in the same form as that illustrated in Plates 124-126, but in this case there is a conventional blue ground, characteristic of many other MIST-type pieces. It, too, bears the same commemorative sprig relief portraits of Washington and La Fayette as on the examples in Plates 124-126 and must, therefore, also have been made specifically for the American market, in order to celebrate the latter's return visit to the United States in August 1824 as an honoured national guest.

The third and extremely interesting feldspathic stoneware piece is illustrated in Plate 174. It is composed of four separate pieces forming a

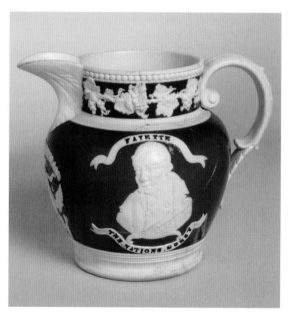

Plate 172. Chetham and Woolley feldspathic stoneware MIST-type jug with portraits of Washington and La Fayette in the same form as illustrated in Plates 124-126. Unmarked. Height 16cm. 1824.

WILLAMS HOUSE, HISTORIC DEERFIELD, USA

tower. The three lower oblong tiers are bevelled at the corners, each with projecting lips, those of the bottom tier in the form of female masks. The upper tier is covered with a pyramidal lid, crowned by a finial in the shape and texture of a woven basket. (The overall construction is almost identical to the central element of a garniture of

Plate 173. Chetham & Woolley helmet shaped feldspathic stoneware jug of the Oak Leaf Border group. Blue edged,with long and short leaf relief moulded decoration in green and blue around the shoulder. Unmarked. Height 16cm. 1795 -1805. PRIVATE COLLECTION, USA

Plate 174. Feldspathic stoneware tower composed of three oblong bevel–edged tiers and a pyramidal cover with a basket shaped finial. Finely decorated with pastel ground colours and superbly executed landscape enamel painting to the main face of each of the tiers and the cover. Height c.39cm. c.1810. Unmarked. PRIVATE COLLECTION. HISTORIC DEERFIELD, USA.

Plate 175. Fine decoration of faces at corners of bottom tier.

five feldspathic stoneware vases which bear the impressed mark 'WOOLLEY' in the Glaisher Collection (Ref:1266-1266d) at the Fitzwilliam Museum Cambridge. These items are illustrated in Hampson, Pl. 25, p.197 and both illustrated and discussed in the *Transactions of the English Ceramic Circle*, Vol.18, Pt. 3, p.561, Fig. 19.)

The whole composition is exquisitely decorated. The main structural features of the tower are highlighted in pastel shades of green and yellow ground, outlined with black and blue edging and enhanced by delicately drawn black foliate lining. The larger front panels of the three oblong tiers and the front panel of the lid are each painted with landscape scenes of the highest artistry. The back and side panels are undecorated other than for single colour grounds edged in black. The high quality of enamel decoration is typified in the treatment of the moulded faces at the corners of the bottom tier shown in Plate 175.

An unmarked tower of almost identical construction to that shown in Plate 174, including the basket-shaped finial, but of porcelain, highly gilded and with flower decorated panels, is known in Temple Newsam House collection, Leeds. Further discussion of this piece and also a set of three tiers of an incomplete similar tower, again of porcelain, has been conducted in recent newsletters of the Northern Ceramic Society (No.s 155 & 156). The tiers of the latter piece are also decorated with landscapes. It is argued there that the ceramic painter William Billingsley was responsible for the decoration of this incomplete porcelain tower, an attribution claimed partly because of the close similarity of the painting of fruit on one of the panels to fruit decoration known on a Pinxton jug.

Close examination of the feldspathic stoneware body of the Deerfield tower has led me to conclude that it has the characteristics of the body perfected by the Chetham & Woolley enterprise. Also the decorative palette is very like that found on Chetham & Woolley ware; the yellow akin to the shade found at the neck of the jug illustrated in Plate 52 and the pink tint found in the landscape skies a hallmark feature of landscape decoration on other Chetham & Woolley wares. As has been mentioned earlier, it is difficult to know whether all Chetham & Woolley enamel decoration was conducted in-house, and indeed it is quite possible that there were many highly accomplished ceramic artists active in the industry of the time whose names have not survived. However, there is an intriguing comment in the letter quoted in Note 57 that after his bankruptcy Richard Woolley was encouraged to seek his living by 'ornamenting the Milan earthenware'. For such a suggestion to have been made implies that he did not lack talent in this respect.

APPENDIX 1

Sprig Relief Decoration: Method

All types of dry-bodied stoneware have representative examples of sprig relief decoration. Wedgwood jasperware is probably the best recognised form of the sprig relief decorated stoneware genre. In this case the white relief stoneware decoration, often in the form of classical figures, is presented against a coloured background stoneware body, most famously Wedgwood Blue. The method of making sprig relief decoration for all dry-bodied stonewares was essentially the same as that used in the manufacture of Wedgwood jasperware.

The procedure was as follows:

1. First, a relief model of the required design was made. Many of the original models commissioned by Josiah Wedgwood were fashioned in wax. Some examples of these survive at the Wedgwood Museum Trust.[1] Wax seems to have been a widely used modelling material for the original design subjects. It was also possible to use the bas relief figures on existing objects, such as the Portland Vase, as models.

2. An intaglio plaster mould was cast from the original model.*

3. From the intaglio plaster mould, a relief cast was taken in a ceramic material which was subsequently fired to a hard biscuit body. In the firing process the relief cast shrank by between a sixth and a seventh, meaning it was always important for the original model to be made sufficiently large. It was possible to reduce the size of a relief cast by successive firings: a second and smaller intaglio plaster mould could be made from the first biscuit cast which had already been reduced by firing. From this second mould a new relief cast could be made in the ceramic material which again would shrink by a sixth or a seventh when fired to a biscuit hardness. By repeating this process the size of the relief cast could be successively reduced without loss of detail. Conversely, the size of a relief cast could not be increased.

4. Working moulds in plaster of Paris were taken from the biscuit relief cast. Often designs would be broken into sections so that individual working moulds might reproduce only a part of the whole design. These individual moulds are commonly referred to as 'sprig moulds'.

5. The unfired stoneware body was pressed into the intaglio plaster moulds and when it was nearly dry, the resulting relief 'sprig' would be picked out and placed carefully with a little clay slip (see Appendix 4) onto the unfired surface to be decorated.

6. A single firing produced a sprig relief decorated item of ware.

*Josiah Wedgwood refers to the second of these procedures when writing to Sir William Hamilton on 24 June 1786 concerning the Portland Vase: 'Most of the figures [on the vase] have their surfaces partially decayed by time. When we mould from these figures.' (MS. E.18976-26)

APPENDIX 2

Genealogy of Antony Chetham & Elaine Chetham (Née Marr)

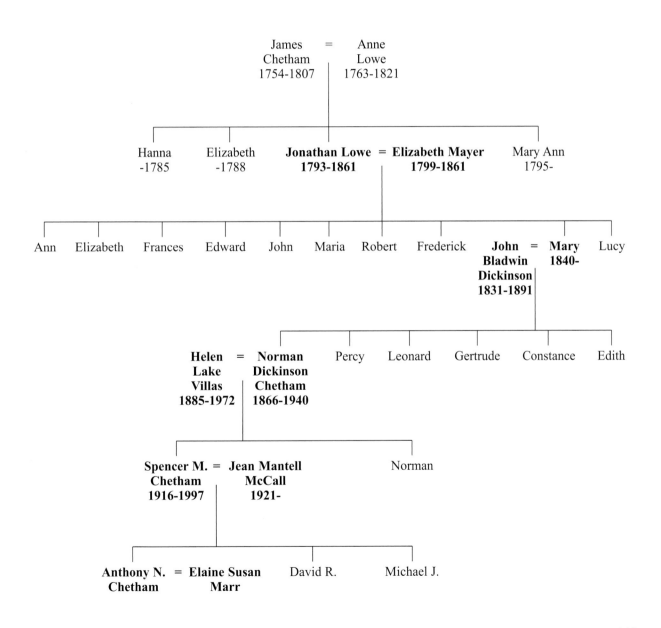

APPENDIX 3

Turning and Engine Turning

From the early eighteenth century turning and engine turning, which appeared later in the 1760s, were two processes widely used to finish and decorate wares by the manufacturers of all types of stoneware; these bodies seemed particularly receptive materials for engine turning.[2] The available evidence suggests that the engine turning technique was first developed in Staffordshire by Josiah Wedgwood and later adopted more widely by other stoneware potters. The original ideas for the engine turning machine may have come to Wedgwood from the Soho factory of Matthew Boulton, the famous Birmingham manufacturer. There are accounts that Wedgwood had first heard of an engine turning lathe at the Soho factory in 1763,[3] but it is not known when he actually installed his own apparatus. However in a letter to Thomas Bentley of February 1767 Wedgwood writes: 'We shall want the book on Engine turning with us...'[4] and in a second letter of 23 May 1767 he appears excited by a machine he had just seen at Soho which may perhaps have been an improved engine turning device.[5] In an account of his travels in 1771, Young confirms both the high wage rates of 'Engine lath men' and states that 'Mr Wedgwood was the first person who introduced this machine'.[6]

(a) Turning

Turning was a method of finishing a ceramic piece after throwing, but before the item had become too dry (a stage generally referred to as 'leather hardness'). The turning process could be carried out on a rotating lathe with the article mounted horizontally or, in the case of items such as large jugs, inverted on the potter's wheel and shaved with appropriate tools against various templates. Whilst rotating, different tools were brought into contact with the surface of the vessel to pare down the walls or create steps, rings, etc.

(b) Engine Turning

Engine turning is a more developed form of a simple turning lathe. In this case the lathe is operated with an eccentric motion which makes it possible to cut elaborate patterns into the leather-hard subject; the more complicated cuts were made with the aid of a guided tool called a rosette. By this means fluted, diced, and other intricate geometric patterns could be cut into a leather-hard ceramic body. Engine turned decorative patterns were generally applied to the lower portion of a stoneware piece in a band above the foot, but in some cases almost the whole item is decorated in this way.

APPENDIX 4

Slip Casting

The term Slip Casting describes a technique used for manufacturing hollow ceramic wares. In his *History of Staffordshire* from 1688, Dr Plot wrote: 'These [clays] mixed with water they make into a consistence thinner than syrup, so that being put into a bucket it will run out through a quill: this they call slip...'

In the first part of the process the slip is poured into a plaster of Paris mould, the walls of which have been shaped around a model of the required item. The plaster of Paris mould absorbs water from the slip, leaving against the mould walls a thin layer of clay. (The particles of this clay were previously suspended in the water from the slip which was absorbed by the plaster of Paris.) Up to the point of saturation of the plaster of Paris, the longer the slip is left in the mould, the more water is absorbed and the thicker will be the layer of clay adhering to the mould walls. When the layer of clay against the mould walls is thick enough, the surplus slip is poured off and out of the mould. The clay cast against the walls of the mould is then left to dry until it reaches a 'leather-hard' state within the mould. In so doing the clay casting shrinks to such an extent that it becomes smaller than the plaster of Paris mould and this makes it easier to extract the casting.

APPENDIX 5

James Underwood Mist

The link between James Mist (a London retailer with premises at 82 Fleet Street) and the factories of Lane End was the outcome of an earlier association which had originated with Andrew Abbott. The latter was originally a Dorset man who, in about 1760, when he was seventeen or eighteen, set out for London to find work. He was soon employed 'gilding black tea ware' and later moved to work in a creamware (Queen's ware) warehouse in Thomas Street.

By 1780 Andrew Abbottt was in a position to purchase admission to the freedom of the City of London, an essential pre-requisite for all who wished to trade within the City boundaries. The Chamberlain's record of his admission read: 'Andrew Abbott of Fleet Street, London, chinaman and Potter, made free by redemption, the fifth day of December 1780'.

Freedom of the City of London could only be obtained through one of the City livery companies and only by one of the three ways: by patrimony, by apprenticeship or by redemption (purchase). Abbott was admitted by the third method as a member of the Carpenters' Company. This does not imply he was a carpenter – belonging to one of the companies was simply a condition of admittance.

Shortly afterwards Bailey's *Northern Directory* of 1781 has the following entry: 'Turner and Abbott, Staffordshire potters and glass men, 9, Old Fish Street in London'. The 'Turner' mentioned here was John Turner a well established and respected Lane End potter. He

had clearly entered into partnership with Mr Abbott in order to establish a trading outlet in London. In 1782 Turner and Abbott moved their premises from Old Fish Street to 81 Fleet Street. By 1783 they had also taken over 82 Fleet Street as their principal showroom. Here they offered 'any kind of Staffordshire ware made to pattern, and neatly enamelled with ciphers, crests, coats of arms or any other device.'

Within an advertisement in the *Morning Herald and Daily Advertiser* of 31 January 1785 it was claimed: 'They likewise manufacture a very general assortment of Egyptian Black, and Bamboo or Cane colour Teapots, some elegantly mounted with silver spouts and chains and Mugs and Jugs with silver rims and covers...'

It is probable that Abbott had no direct connection with manufacturing at Turner's Lane End Factory. It may be that it was considered beneficial to give the impression that the London outlet was the retailing arm of a manufacturing business, and that would have been the case for Turner.

On 21 December 1787 John Turner died and his two sons William and John took control of the substantial Lane End manufacturing business. They also maintained the London partnership with Andrew Abbott. Although in February 1788 the Turner brothers had inherited three fifths of the London partnership, they subsequently drew heavily on this capital and their share was soon diminished to one third. In August 1792 they sold their holding to the other partners, Andrew

Abbott and Benjamin Newbury, who had been introduced some time previously.

Although they had relinquished all ownership of the London business, William and John Turner nevertheless continued to trade with it. Andrew Abbott also sold the wares of other manufacturers including Chetham & Woolley. Unfortunately the financial circumstances of the Turner brothers did not improve and they were declared bankrupt in July 1806.

In 1802, Andrew Abbott had dissolved his connection with Benjamin Newbury and he then traded as sole proprietor for nearly four years. In March 1806, when Abbott was sixty-three and perhaps contemplating retirement, he entered into a new partnership with James Underhill Mist. The latter appears to have had no prior experience of the china trade, but he came from a relatively wealthy background and could probably provide capital. James Underhill Mist was descended from a well established London family of brass founders and was only twenty-two when he went into partnership with Abbott.[7]

The relationship between Richard Abbott and James Mist appears not to have been easy, perhaps partly due to their discrepancies in age. In March 1809, after just three years, Andrew Abbott withdrew from the partnership. James Mist, then aged twenty-five, became the sole proprietor, though he leased part of the Fleet Street premises from Abbott. The residual relationship and settlement of affairs between Abbott and Mist was difficult and acrimonious. In November 1814 it culminated with Abbott instructing his solicitors to take legal action against James Mist. By this time James Mist was already in severe financial difficulty – a state of affairs which appears to have begun to develop at least two years previously – and on 29 April 1815 he was declared bankrupt.

An important aspect of these various events is that although James Mist had been operating from the Fleet Street premises since March 1806, with Abbott as his partner, it was not until March 1809 that he took sole control. There are some examples of Chetham & Woolley feldspathic stoneware which are impressed with the 'MIST' mark in various formats (marked pieces of other makers' wares are also known). However, during the period of partnership it is unlikely that Abbott would have allowed James Mist to mark items of ware with his name alone. Therefore, any items of ware bearing the 'MIST' mark are likely to have been made between March 1809 and Mist's bankruptcy in April 1815, the six years during which he traded as the sole proprietor.

In addition to the Chetham & Woolley items, mostly decorative pieces marked 'MIST', there are many more which are in exactly the same form and style. The generic term MIST-type is used to describe these unmarked examples. Given the narrow span for the dating of 'MIST' marked pieces, the implication is that they were made at the Lane End Commerce Street site when Ann Chetham was in sole control. Unmarked pieces would also have been made during this time and also in the periods of preceding Chetham & Woolley partnerships involving James and Ann Chetham and Richard Woolley.

Several manufacturers are known to have supplied James Mist. For example William, one of the bankrupt sons of John Turner, quickly re-established himself in business and he certainly supplied Mist with a special patented stone chinaware. The mark 'Turner. Mist Sole Agent' appears on rare examples of willow pattern plates of this material. Unfortunately, however, William Turner's re-established business was not long-lived. In January 1813 he failed to deliver an order to Mist and by September 1814 the premises of Turner's new business were for sale.[8]

APPENDIX 6

Chetham & Woolley Factory

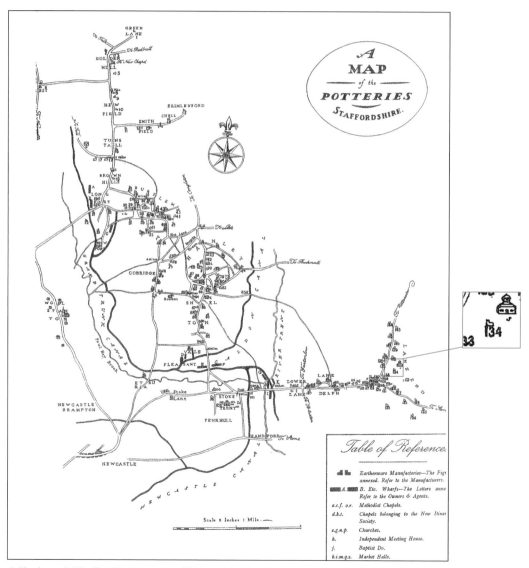

Chetham & Woolley Factory is no. 134.

APPENDIX 7

Plate 177. Central vase of garniture. Height: 38.5cm.

In the Postscript reference has been made to the central element of a garniture of five vases in the Glaisher Collection of the Fitzwilliam Museum, Cambridge. These are illustrated in Plate 176.

There is a striking similarity between the 'tower' illustrated in Plate 174 and the central element of the garniture in Plate 176. It has been generally assumed that the garniture, impress marked 'WOOLLEY' was made by Richard Woolley when he occupied the Turner factory premises during the brief period of his independent enterprise there (see page 19). On the face of it, this is the obvious conclusion to draw.

However, the elaborate technical quality of the Fitzwilliam Museum garniture suggests well-developed and well-functioning production facilities. Whilst these may have been available at the Turner premises when Richard Woolley occupied them in 1809, this might equally be thought unlikely since, following the Turner brothers' bankruptcy in 1806, the works had presumably not been active for three years. Bringing a previously defunct factory back to life might not have been swiftly achieved; surviving evidence shows that Richard Woolley became bankrupt in a very short space of time.

Since it is now known from Elaine Chetham's important genealogical work that Richard Woolley and Anne Chetham were brother and sister, it is not inconceivable that the garniture might have been made when they worked together at the Commerce Street site from 1807 to 1809. In this brief period, the simple 'WOOLLEY' mark – their family name – would not have been entirely out of place. However, it must be stressed that there is no evidence to support such a speculation other than the highly accomplished appearance of the garniture itself.

Plate 176. A garniture of five vases in the MIST-type style. Sprig relief decorated with classical sprigs and putti. Impress marked 'WOOLLEY', 1805-1810.

FITZWILLIAM MUSEUM, CAMBRIDGE. GLAISHER COLLECTION

NOTES

INTRODUCTION

1. Wedgwood MS: Ref: L1116/22237, 16 November 1791. It is not clear exactly what materials or products were delivered, at this period the use of wooded hogsheads was common practice in the shipment of ceramic goods.

2. Universal British Directory, 1791-c.1797.
3. See Map p.118.

4. J.Allbut & Son, *The Staffordshire Pottery Directory*, Hanley, 1802.

5. John Robinson joined the founder's son, Jonathan Lowe Chetham, in 1822 and the title Chetham and Robinson was used at some point. The mark 'C & R' is known on earthenwares. John Robinson's son, Samuel, joined the firm in 1834, but appears to have left following his father's death in 1840.

6. See: Edwards and Hampson.

7. See: Edwards and Hampson.

8. For explanations of kiln temperatures required for stoneware production, see: Rhodes; G.W. Elliott in Lockett and Halfpenny 1982, pp. 9-13; Edwards and Hampson p.49.

9. See: Appendix 1.

10. Since all stonewares of this period shared similar manufacturing procedures, the use of a common method of decoration is perhaps unsurprising. However it is likely that care must have been taken to maintain separate batches of moulds where a single manufacturer, made both black basalt and honey coloured or even lighter stonewares, both bodies decorated with the same sprig relief decoration. Contamination of the lighter wares by black basalt, for example, would have been possible in the absence of segregation of the sprig moulds involved.

11. Wedgwood letter to Bentley 14 January, 1776:

'I believe I can now assure you of a conquest, & a very important one to us. No less than the firing our fine Jasper & Onyx with as much certainty as our basalts or black ware...'

But Josiah Wedgwood's confidence was premature. He wrote again on 6 June, 1776:

'The Jasper is the most delicately whimsical of any substance I ever engag'd with; & as such unavoidable losses attend it, we must endeavour to make the living pay for the dead.'

12. Wedgwood letter to Bentley 1 September 1778:

'To make the most of this tour I have two or three very fine tablets with me, & an easy introduction to show them at Kedleston ... Lady Bagot fixed upon a tablet & two frises & wished Ld. Scarsdale might see some of the tablets... Depend upon it they must sell...'

13. Wedgwood had many prestigious agents dealing on his behalf in continental Europe. C.C.H. Rost in Leipzig, for example, sold to Prince Friedrich von Anhalt-Dessau. See: Edwards and Hampson, p.105.

14. For example, Wedgwood to Bentley, from London, 6 February, 1769:

'Etruscan Vases are the run at present ... I sho'd be glad to have ... the Duchess of Bedfords Vases, as I scarcely dare see her Grace without them.'

And Later on the same day:

'My last, & best chap was Ld. Bessborough ... admires our vases & manufacture prodigiously ... & that he will do me every service in his power'

For a discussion of Wedgwood's term 'Etruscan', see: Reilly, vol.1, p.398.

15. Wedgwood letter to Bentley 21st November 1768: 'Bass reliefs will have a most fine effect too, & will fetch Guineas instead of shillings'. See also Appendix 1.

16. With Jasperware it appears Wedgwood did have a period of monopoly. Wedgwood letter to Bentley, 5 July, 1776: 'nobody, besides W. & B., can make Jasper'.

17. See: Hillier, p.15.

18. See: Hillier, p.17.

19. For accounts of manufacturers of dry-bodied stoneware at this period, see: Edwards and Hampson.

2. MARKET CONDITIONS

1. Thomas estimates that those employed in the Potteries had risen steadily from approximately 7,500 in 1785 to approximately 20,000 by 1835. See: John Thomas, 12-13.

2. See: Sloan, *Enlightenment*, British Museum Press, 2003, pp. 70-79.

3. In France the new dominance of reason in world of ideas was recognised and expressed by d'Alembert, the co-author with Diderot of the *Encyclopedie* (*Dictionnaire Raisonne des Sciences, des Arts, et des Metiers*), the first volume of which was printed in 1751. In 1759 he wrote:

'A most remarkable change in our ideas is taking place, one of such rapidity that it seems that there is the promise of greater change still to come. It will be for the future to decide the aim, the nature and the limits of this revolution, the drawbacks and disadvantages of which posterity will be better able to judge than we can.'

4. Vide, *Bacon's Novum Organum*, and also passages within *The New Atlantis*. See also: Hill, p. 88.

5. See: Berlin, pp.18, 30-112, 115-161, 162-260.

6. It is estimated that the population in England and Wales in 1700 was 5,800,000 and by 1750 it had risen to 6,250,000. By the Census of 1801 it had reached 9,192,810 and by the second Census in 1831 it was 14,070,681. See : Beales, pp. 68-69.
There were those at the time who thought the population was growing to an unsustainable degree. Thomas Malthus wrote in 1803:

'A man who is born into a world already possessed, if he cannot get subsistence from his parents on whom he has a just demand, and if society do not want his labour, has no claim of right to the smallest portion of food, and, in fact, has no business to be where he is. At nature's mighty feast there is no vacant cover for him.' See: Malthus, p.531.

7. See: Uglow. The Lunar Society was centred on Birmingham and its satellite conurbations. It was a loosely formed association of like minded friends with common interests in largely scientific and technical matters. They met at each other's houses once a month at the time of the full moon, which provided the best light for members to travel back to their homes. The small membership included such eminent persons as Matthew Boulton, James Watt, Joseph Priestley, Josiah Wedgwood and Erasmus Darwin.

8. Despite this, the second half of the eighteenth century was a period of great variation in the yields of the soil due to climatic factors; prices for produce remained high. See: Ashton (3), p.62.

9. See: Berg (2), p.293 and Andrews.

Diary of John Byng, later the fifth Viscount Torrington, 4 June 1792 (Vol.3, p.33):

'My opinion holds, that the labourer has quitted the country, and the Enclosing Acts have in a great measure been the cause. But I shall be answer'd by "think you not that our population is as great as formerly?" "Why, aye, in many counties where manufactures flourish, I think it is, but they have sucked up the villages and single cottages; Birmingham, Manchester and Sheffield swarm with inhabitants…'

On 24 June 1792, (Vol.3, p.114) he continued:

'All around Rochdale they are building away – and have swell'd it from a small market town into a great city...'

10. Ibid, p.114.

'In places where wealth is procured, it is ignorantly spent: for the upstart man of riches knows no better…'

11. The great social changes were affecting long entrenched conceptions of social status. On 22 March 1776 the diarist

James Boswell visited Mathew Boulton's factory at Soho near Birmingham. He record the event as follows:

'Boulton seemed to me a clever fine fellow. I regretted that I did not know mechanics well enough to comprehend the description of machines lately invented by him... We drank tea with him and Mrs. Boulton. I was struck with the thought of a smith being a great man. Here I saw it... He was a sort of iron chieftain'.

12. See: Berg (2), p.27 onwards.

13. In July 1787 Josiah Wedgwood made an arrangement for Henry Webber (1754-1826) to travel to Rome to manage a group of artists there who were to work on his behalf. See: Gaye Blake-Roberts in Walford and Young, 'English Ceramic Design', *The English Ceramic Circle*, 2003, p.116.
The principle of the division of labour was not an original notion. The idea was inherent in a passage from as long ago as Xenophon who wrote as follows in his Cyropaedia:

'...In a small city the same man must make beds and chairs and ploughs and tables, and often build houses as well: and indeed he will be only too glad if he can find enough employers in all trades to keep him. Now it is impossible that a single man working at a dozen crafts can do them all well; but in the great cities, owing to the wide demand for each particular thing, a single craft will suffice for a means of livelihood, and often enough even a single department of that; there are shoe-makers who will only make sandals for men and others only for women. Or one artisan will get his living merely by stitching shoes, another by cutting them out, a third by shaping the upper leathers, and a fourth will do nothing but fir the parts together. Necessarily the man who spends all his time and trouble on the smallest task will do that task the best...'

Also it appears that in China the division of labour had long been practised in the manufacture of ceramics. From 1736 to 1753 Tang Ying was the mandarin in charge of porcelain manufacture in the province of Jiangxi, which includes Jingdezhen. In 1743 he wrote a text entitled *Twenty Illustrations of the Manufacture of Porcelain*. In this, he reveals how separate sub-functions of labour were organised to produce complete articles of ceramic ware.

14. A facsimile of the library list is printed in the *7th Wedgwood International Seminar Publication*, Chicago 1962, p.60.

15. See: Hillier, ibid, p.74. The sale was held at the house of William Turner on 25 and 26 May, 1813
Turner's books were listed as including amongst others:

'*Hamiltion's Antiquities*, 4 vols., *Herculaneum and Etruscan Antiquities*, 7 vols., *Montfaucon's Antiquities*, 5 vols., *Plaw's Architecture, Italian Views, Beceuil*'. It is likely that it also contained: the Compte de Caylus's *Receuil d'Antiquites egyptiennes, etrusques, greques, romaines, et gauloises*, 6 Volumes, 1752 -1755.

16. From as early as the 1770s Josiah Wedgwood had employed John Flaxman (1755-1826), perhaps as a result of connections with his father, a plastercast maker in London. John Flaxman expressed a desire to go to Rome and it was probably partly through his regular commissions for the Wedgwood factory in the 1780s that he was eventually able to make the journey in 1787. See: Bindman, p.47. See also: Berg (2), p.131.

17. One of Wedgwood's most important modellers was William Hackwood (1757-1839). Having been hired in1769 as an 'ingenious boy', he later became chief modeller of ornamental works. Josiah much appreciated the value of Hackwood's work and in 1776 he wrote to Bentley wishing he had 'half a dozen more Hackwoods'. In 1776, whilst still only nineteen, Hackwood made a model of the Birth of Bacchus which became the largest jasper tablet so far made. Not all Wedgwood's associations with modellers were a success, however. Voyez was employed by him in 1769, but the association was not a success and the arrangement broke down. Voyez created problems for Wedgwood by spreading adverse rumours amongst customers and later made basalt medallions for his own trade, sometimes perhaps stamped with the Wedgwood and Bentley mark.

18. Wedgewood had showrooms in London, Bath and Dubiln, as well as an extensive network of agents including many in continental Europe. See: Reilly, pp.65-76. See also: Edwards & Hampson, p.105.

19. Country pursuits which had long been enjoyed by the aristocracy and gentry were now becoming available to those prospering in commerce. The first volume of *The Sporting Magazine* was published in 1793.
The 'Address to the Public' in the first edition is noteworthy in its resonance with messages heard in modern times from health clubs, and country sports magazines to office-bound professionals and businessmen:

'To relieve the mind from the fatiguing studies of

the closet, and preserve the human frame from those afflictions which a sedentary life too frequently occasions, recreation and exercise are found to be essential... What exercise then can be equal to that which has athletic rural sports for its object? What exercise can be compared to that in which the mind is pleasingly and anxiously interested concerning the success or failure of an event?'

See also: Leese *Northern Ceramic Society Journal*, vol 5, pp. 61-78.

20. The opening marked Josiah Wedgwood's partnership with Thomas Bentley. The partnership document was dated 10 August 1769.

21. (E.18392-25) See also: Finer and Savage, p.131.

22. See: Whiter, Drakard and Holdway; Lockett and Godden; Furniss and Wagner; Atterbury and Batkin; Godden.

3. DOCUMENTARY RECORD

1. See: Shaw; also Mankowitz and Haggar, p.200.

2. See: Shaw p.225.

3. One point of Simeon Shaw's account of the Chetham & Woolley invention appears to be misleading. The phrase 'without glaze or smear' implies an entirely glaze-free product, but this is contradicted by the contemporary description of the production method given by the potter John Riley, quoted later (Note 17).
This matter is discussed by P. Halfpenny (Lockett and Halfpenny (1) p.109), in which he writes: 'The temperature of the biscuit firing would cause the glaze wash to volatilise and the small quantity would be responsible for the merest hint of sheen noticeable on these wares – a flash.'

4. See: Hollens p.224.

5. *Staffordshire Advertiser*, 22 August, 1807.

6. Litchfield Record Office, Ref B/C/11 1807 James Chetham. The document was found by Mrs Elaine Chetham who is married to Mr Antony Chetham, a direct descendant of James Chetham, the original partner. Mrs Chetham contacted me some years ago to enquire about the study I was making of the Chetham & Woolley factory. She was involved in a genealogical study of her family and neither she nor her husband had at first been aware that the Chetham family had

any connection with the pottery industry. Mr Chetham's direct line of descent from James Chetham is shown in Appendix 2.

7. This information has been provided privately by Mrs Elaine Chetham and comes from her family genealogical research.

8. Ibid.

9. *Staffordshire Advertiser*, 16 December, 1809.

10. See: Hillier, p.72.

11. *Staffordshire Advertiser*, 2 March, 1811.

There is surviving evidence of Richard Woolley's independent period in trade. An elaborate garniture of five vases, each piece impress marked WOOLLEY survives in the Glaisher Collection at the Fitzwilliam Museum, Cambridge. It is illustrated in Hampson Plate 25, p.197.

The consequences of Richard Woolley's business failure were catastrophic for both himself and his family. A long letter in the Sutherland Papers addressed to the Marquis of Stafford from Richard Woolley's son, Samuel, reveals a catalogue of distressing circumstances and events. However, the suggested date for the letter, 1810, does not easily conform to the *Staffordshire Advertiser*'s date of Richard Woolley's bankruptcy. If the date of the letter is correct it perhaps means that Richard Woolley was in financial difficulties within only a few months of quitting his partnership with Ann Chetham and was effectively bankrupt prior to the date of the *Staffordshire Advertiser* announcement.

The letter reads as follows:

The Marquiss of Stafford

When your Lordship has perused these lines perhaps you will be surprised at the audacity of the person who wrote them and at the strangeness of their purport or perhaps your breast will be touched with those soft emotions of pity which the generous and humane (whatever may be their rank in life) ever feel for the miseries and misfortunes of their fellow creatures, God grant this last may be the case and that we may add one more to the innumerable instances of your Lordships goodness in relieving those whom misfortune has brought to the lowest ebb of misery and distress.

Some years ago my Father was a Manufacturer of earthenware in Lane End and his conduct was such as to gain him the confidence and esteem of his acquaintances. he then maintained his family in credit and respectability and was able to render assistance to any of his neighbours which he never failed to do whenever it was necessary, alas how changed the scene in 1810 through the failure of several houses in London and Liverpool and the badness of trade he became a Bankrupt, his affairs however in consequence of the regularity in which they always were kept were soon arranged and his creditors convinced of the honest uprightness of his conduct offered to assist him in any plan he might think it proper to pursue, he accepted their offer and went out with a quantity of Earthenware to Malta where he formed a connexion and had once more a prospect of living in a respectable manner, that prospect however soon blighted, the Plague broke out and the distructive ravages soon compelled the inhabitants to seek safety in flight: some remained to take care of their property and thousands fell victim to the dreadful disease many of the Merchants connected with Malta were completely ruined and amongst them my Father, he called his creditors together and laid the state of his affairs before them and they perfectly satisfied that it was impossible for him to prevent the loss he had sustained with a confidence and humanity that did them honour furnished him with a quantity of goods to go to Gibralta, he went and as there appeared to be a fair opening and sent me out to reside which I did until a malignant fever broke out at Gibraltar Cadiz Malaga and the neighbouring Ports which put a complete stop to all business and the distress it occasioned was inconceivable to any one not connected or from their situation in life free from the care anxiety and uncertainty of Trade. The consequence to me after escaping the disease was the failure of two houses with whom I had considerable dealings and after their affairs were settled and I had collected the remains of my affects I was obliged to return home with about a twentieth part of what I ought to have brought. To attempt to describe the feeling of my Father and family on this distressing occasion would be vain and how to maintain his family he was utterly at a loss to know, but before he could enter into any proceeding for that purpose he had a duty to perform which however painful it might be to his feelings he determined not to swerve from that was to wait upon his creditors and inform them of his situation, I accompanied him and found the (with the exception of one person) so far from having

any intention of adding to his troubles to sympathise in his misfortunes and pity his distress. To assist him further was however out of their power and as he was confident that there was some secret and unforeseen workings in human affairs which continually baffled all his endeavours and as he was determined not to involve either himself or those who had so generously assisted him further than what he had done he endeavoured to procure a situation but this he soon found was impossible as one of his creditors to whom he owed 100th out of an account of 700 threatened to arrest him if he was not paid immediately and as it was quite out of his power to pay the money he accepted of an offer to go to France to see if anything could be made of a mine of clay belonging to an Englishman but as he had not money sufficient to make an undertaking of that kind answer was my Father was advised to go to Milan and endeavour by ornamenting the Milan Earthenware to procure a livelihood for himself and Family which there is no doubt he will be able to accomplish provided my Mother sisters and self were there to assist him but unfortunately we are without the means of going so far, in fact if it were not for the generosity and humanity of a friend with whom we at present lodge we should be obliged to apply to the Parish, our friends are unable to lend us the money to carry us to Milan and the little my Father has been able to send us is expended for our maintenance and we are now literally without a shilling, almost driven to madness by the suffering of my Mother and sisters, utterly at a loss what course to take, and having heard of the many instances of your Lordships goodness and liberality I have come to determination of applying to you trusting that you will pardon my boldness, pity our suffering and relieve our distress. My applying to your Lordship I acknowledge is bold and romantic in the extreme, but when once a thought of doing so entered my imagination I could not divest myself of it and even the most remote prospect of success has created a sensation of pleasure in my breast to which it has long been a Stranger; the idea of relieving the present distress of my Mother and Sisters, of joining my father and ultimately by our joint exertions liquidating the debts we have contracted by the assistance which I hope your lordship will not refuse continually forces itself on my mind.

You may my Lord perhaps observe that you know nothing at all of us and that this may be all a fiction but a little enquiry will convince you that I have stated nothing but the truth. My grand Father lived in your Lordships family Fifty Four years. Would to God my

Father had entered too, he would not then have been taken by American Privateers: he would not have suffered the horrors of a shipwreck and had not the dangers of Plagues to encounter no then he might have lived comfortably and happy and have avoided those misfortunes that have hitherto constantly attended him.

Whatever may be the result of this I sincerely hope that your Lordship will forgive my boldness it is the distress I daily see my Mother and Sisters labouring under and the instances I have heard of your Lordships goodness that make me so and they I trust will be sufficient excuse.

I remain you Lordships most humble servant

Samuel Woolley

Whether or not the Marquis of Stafford responded to the letter is not known.

The *Staffordshire Advertiser* (7 January, 1826) records that Richard Woolley died at Stone on Christmas Day, 1825 aged sixty-one.

12. See: Hampson, p.46.

13. *Staffordshire Advertiser*, 16 June, 1821.

14. T. Albutt, *Newcastle and Pottery Directory 1822-23*.

15. *North Staffordshire Mercury*, 19 September, 1840.

16. *North Staffordshire Mercury*, 30 September and 28 October, 1871.

17. *Journal of Ceramic History*, Vol.13: Ref: Notebook p.45. Some interpretation of the formula is given by P. Halfpenny in *Stonewares and Stone China*, Northern Ceramic Society exhibition catalogue, 1982, p.103. See also: Shaw p.225.

18. *Journal of Ceramic History*, Vol.13: Ref: Notebook p.46.

Feldspar Clay, called Vitrescent

Clay is of three qualities. That which is got at the top burns whitest, has more clay in it and less of the feldspar sand; it is therefore rougher, and is of greater advantage. The next appears to contain a greater proportion of feldspar sand, is a little more vitrifiable, burns pretty nearly as good a colour as the above mentioned, is not so tenacious to work but more valuable in other respects, as with a

proper mixture of other materials it will produce a greater transparency. The third quality will produce a greater and better transparency than the first but is very much inferior in colour, producing, of itself, ware superior to the best cream colour only.

These 3 qualities of Feldspar Clay have a contrary effect, on being burned, to all other clays. All other Clays burn very much browner by very hard fire, but the Vitrescent or feldspar Clay burn much whiter when vitrified, than before vitrification. The same effect is observable with respect to Feldspar. It burns much whiter when completely vitrified and the transparency greater and finer, than when fired with a less degree of heat. A china biscuit fire produces by far the best colour and transparency.

19. See: Hollens p.224.

20. Eatwell and Werner, 'A London Staffordshire Warehouse. 1794-1825', *Northern Ceramic Society Journal*, Vol.8, 1991, p.91.

21. *Staffordshire Advertiser*, 20 September, 1851.

22. The tiles were discovered by Mrs E. Chetham.

4. THE OAK-LEAF BORDER GROUP

1. City Museum & Art Gallery, Stoke-on-Trent, item ref: 152P1962.

2. The cover is not a perfect fit and the possibility that it was provided as a later 'marriage' has been questioned. The matter remains unresolved.

3. For illustrated examples of the borders on the wares of various makers see: Edwards (1) & (2), Edwards & Hampson, and Grant.

4. The author met the gentleman who had discovered the shards and he very kindly provided detailed information concerning his find. It appears that a Lockett business occupied the Chancery Lane site from 1822-1858. See: Hampson p.107.

5. An account of the factory and an illustration of a Samuel Hollens Venus and Cupid finial is found in Burton (1) p.152.

6. Robertshaw: *Northern Ceramic Society Newsletter* No.54,1984. Also Emmerson 'British Teapots and Tea Drinking', *Her Majesty's Stationary Office*, 1992, p.160.

7. For a critical review of this and other finials see Dr & Mrs Leonard Rackow 'The Sybil and The Widow', *Transactions of The English Ceramic Circle*, 1984, Vol 11, p.163.

8. The coffee pots in Plates 17 and 18 were originally in private collections in the UK.

5. PEARL DRY JUGS

1. See: Lockett and Halfpenny (1) p.109. For illustrated examples see: Edwards and Hampson.

2. See: Smith p.41 and illustrations 93-96.

3. See: Note 11, p.121.

4. See: Lewis, p.158.

7. PRATT TYPE WARES

1. Lewis, J. and G., *Pratt Ware*, Antique Collectors' Club, 1984, p.13.

8. MIST-TYPE WARES

1. Merseyside Museum Collection, Ref: 18.11.25.4.

2. Blakey, 'Turner–type stonewares and James Mist', *Northern Ceramic Society Newsletter* No.85, 1992.

3. This is a term which appears to have been first given to the decorative feature by auctioneers. See: Phillips Auctioneers, London: Sale, 23 January 2001, Lots 54 and 58.

4. See: Hollens, *Transactions of the English Ceramic Circle,* Vol II, 1989, Plate 116(a) and Miller and Berthoud, *An Anthology of British Teapots*, Plate 1003.

5. For a list of some the designs used for wares of this type see Hildyard, 'Country Classical', *Antique Collecting*, September 1997 p.12.

6. There is an example of a MIST-type mug with the Wellington and Blucher portraits in the collection of the Fitzwilliam Museum, Cambridge.

7. Howarth, J., 'Andrew Abbott and the Fleet Street Partnership', *Northern Ceramic Society Journal*, 1996, Vol. 3, p.110.

9. MISCELLANEOUS

1. The head illustrated in 156 is in the Schreiber Collection in the Victoria and Albert Museum, London, Catalogue No.573. It is described as follows:

> 'Bust of Cupid. White stoneware with slight glaze, painted in colours. Square pedestal, on each side of which are oval panels outlined in pink; the front panel is blank; the others have reliefs of (1) Cupid with two doves billing, (2) a Muse crowning the bust of a poet, (3) a woman pouring out a libation. Blue lines round the top and bottom of the plinth. Height 10inches. LIVERPOOL. (HERCULANEUM POTTERY); about 1800.

2. See Hillier (2) Illustrations 14-21 and p.47.

3. One is in the Victoria and Albert Museum, London and the other in the Scottish Military Museum, Edinburgh.

4. See Chaffers, Vol.2, p.113.

APPENDICES

1. Gaye Blake–Roberts in Walford and Young 'English Ceramic Design 1600-2002', *The English Ceramic Circle*, 2003 , pp. 115–121.

2. In 1750 Thomas Whieldon paid for 'turning' at the 'skilled' labour rate (see Berg M. (2) p.135.

3. Reilly Vol. 1 p.306.

4. MS E-1837-25.

5. MS E-18147-25.

6. Young A., Vol. 3, p.254.

7. There is a brass chandelier in the parish church of Wollaston, Northamptonshire, with the inscription 'Mist Long Acre fecit 1777'. In 1780 his father, James, had married (at St Phillips Church in Birmingham) Mary Underhill, whose father, Thomas Underhill, was also a successful Birmingham brass founder, but later retired to farm at Handsworth.

8. Howarth, 'Andrew Abbott and the Fleet Street Partnership', *Northern Ceramic Society Journal*, Vol. 13, p.75.

CONCLUSION

1. Shaw, Simeon, *The History of the Staffordshire Potteries*, G. Jackson, Hanley, 1829.

BIBLIOGRAPHY

Andrews, C. Bruyn, ed., *The Torrington Diaries*, Methuen, 1970

Ashton, T.S. (1), *The Industrial Revolution 1760-1830*, Oxford University Press, 1948

Ashton, T.S. (2), *An Economic History of England: The 18th Century*, Methuen, 1959

Ashton, T.S. (3) *Economic Fluctuations in England 1700-1800*, Oxford University Press, 1959

Atterbury and Batkin, *The Dictionary of Minton*, Antique Collectors' Club, 1990

Beales, H.L., *The Industrial Revolution 1759-1850*, Frank Cass & Co. Ltd., 1958

Berg, Maxine (1), *The Age of Manufactures 1700-1820*, Routledge, 1994

Berg, Maxine (2), *Luxury and Pleasure in Eighteenth Century Britain*, Oxford, 2005

Berlin, Isiah, *The Age of Enlightenment: The 18th Century Philosophers.*, Houghton, Mifflin Co., 1956

Bindman, David, ed., *John Flaxman, R.A.* (Exhibition Catalogue), Royal Academy of Arts, 1979

Burton, William (1), *A History and Description of English Earthenware and Stoneware*, Cassell, 1904

Burton, William (2), *Porcelain its Nature Art and Manufacture*, Batsford, London, 1906

Drakard and Holdway, *Spode Printed Wares*, Longman Group Ltd., 1983

Edwards and Hampson, *English Dry-Bodied Stoneware: Wedgwood and Contemporary Manufacturers 1774-1830*, Antique Collectors' Club, 1998

Edwards, Diana (1), *Black Basalt, Wedgwood and Contemporary Manufacturers*, Antique Collectors' Club, 1994

Chaffers, William, *Marks and Monograms on Pottery and Porcelain*, Reeves, 15th edition, 1965

Edwards, Diana (2), *Neale Pottery and Porcelain: Its predecessors and Successors 1763-1820,* Barrie & Jenkins, 1987

Edwards Roussel, Diana, *The Castleford Pottery 1790-1821*, Wakefield Historical Publications, 1982

Finer and Savage, *The Selected Letters of Josiah Wedgwood*, Cory, Adams & Mackay, 1965

Furniss and Wagner, *Adams Ceramics, Staffordshire Poatters and Pots, 1799-1998*, Schiffer Publishing Ltd., 1999

Godden, Geoffrey, *Ridgway Porcelains*, Antique Collectors' Club, 1985

Grant, Captain M.H., *The Makers of Black Basaltes*, Holland Press, 1910

Hampson, Rodney, 'Longton Potters 1700-1865', *Journal of Ceramic History* Vol. 14, Stoke-on-Trent City Museum and Art Gallery, 1990

Hartwell, R.M., *Causes of the Industrial Revolution in England*, London, 1967

Hill, Christopher, *Intellectual Origins of the English Revolution*, Oxford, 1965

Hillier, Bevis (1), *Master Potters of the Industrial Revolution: The Turners of Lane End*, Cory, Adam & Mackay, 1965

Hillier, Bevis (2), *Pottery and Porcelain 1700-1914*, Weidenfeld and Nicolson, 1968

Hollens, David, 'Some Researches into the Makers of Dry Bodies', *Transactions of the English Ceramic Circle*, Vol. 11, p.224, 1983

Hope, Thomas, *Costumes of the Ancients*, William Miller, London, 1812

Klingender, Francis, *Art and the Industrial Revolution*, Evelyn, Adams and McKay, 1947

Leese, Maureen, 'The Turner Moulds', *Northern Ceramic Society Journal*, 1984, Vol. 5, p.61

Lewis, John and Griselda, *Pratt Ware*, Antique Collectors' Club, 1984

Liang, Miaotai, '*Ming Qing Jingderzhen chengshi jingji yanjiu*' [*Study on urban economics of Jingderzhen in the Ming and Qing periods*], Nanchang: Jiangxi renmin chubanshe, 1991

Lockett and Godden, *Davenport China, Earthenware & Glass 1794–1887*, Barrie & Jenkins, 1989

Lockett and Halfpenny (1), *Creamware and Pearlware*, Stoke-on-Trent City Museum and Art Gallery, 1986

Lockett and Halfpenny (2), *Stonewares and Stone China of Northern England to 1851*, Stoke-on-Trent City Museum and Art Gallery, 1982

Malthus, T. Robert, 'An Essay on the Principle of Population', 1803

Mankowitz W. and Haggar R., *The Concise Encyclopedia of English Pottery and Porcelain*, Andre Deutsch, 1957

McKendrick, Brewer and Plumb, *The Birth of a Consumer Society Europe*, London, 1982

Miller P. and Berthoud M., *An Anthology of British Teapots*, Micawber Publications, 1985

Moll-Murata, Christine, *Guilds and Apprenticeship in China and Europe: The Ceramics Industries of Jingderzhen and Delft*, June 2008

Musson A. and Robinson E., *Science and Technology in the Industrial Revolution*, Gordon and Breach, 1969

Nef, John, *The Cultural Foundation of Industrial Civilization*, Cambridge, 1958

Reilly, Robin, *Wedgwood*, Macmillan, 1989

Reynolds, Sir Joshua, *Discourses on Art*, Yale University Press Edition, 1975

Rhodes, Daniel, *Stoneware and Porcelain: The Art of High Fired Pottery*, Pitman Publishing, 1960

Rouet, Philippe, *Approaches to the Study of Attic Vases*, Oxford, 2001

Shaw, Simeon, *The History of the Staffordshire Potteries*, G. Jackson, Henley, 1829

Sloan, Kim ed., *Enlightenment: Discovering the World in the Eighteenth Century*, The British Museum Press, 2003

Smith, Alan, *Liverpool Herculaneum Pottery*, Barrie & Jenkins, 1970

Thomas, John, *The Rise of the Staffordshire Potteries*, Adams and Dart, 1971

Towner, Donald C., *English Cream-coloured Earthenware*, Faber and Faber, 1957

Uglow, Jenny, *The Lunar Men: The Friends Who Made The Future 1730-1810*, Faber and Faber, 2002

Walford and Massey eds., 'Creamware and Pearlware Re-examined', *English Ceramic Circle*, 2007

Walford and Young, Editors, 'English Ceramic Design 1600-2002', *The English Ceramic Circle*, 2003

Watkin, David, *Thomas Hope and the Neo-Classical Idea*, Murray, 1968

Weatherill, Lorna, *The Pottery Trade and North Staffordshire 1660-1760*, Manchester University Press, 1971

Wedgwood 7th International Seminar Publication, Chicago, 1962

Whiter, Leonard, *Spode: a History of the Family, Factory and Wares from 1733 to 1833*, Barrie & Jenkins, London, 1970

Wyman, Colin, 'The Stoneware of Chetham & Woolley c.1795-c.1820', *Transactions of The English Ceramic Circle*, Vol. 18., 2003, p.208

Young, Arthur, *Six Months Tour Through the North of England*, London, 1769

Young and Jenkins, *The Victoria History of the County of Stafford*, Vol. VIII, London, 1897. (Now maintained by Keele University.)

Xenophon (431-355 BC), *Cyropaedia: the Education of Cyrus*

INDEX

Numbers in **bold** refer to mentions in plates and captions.